P9-CQS-982

The Gift of Great Poetry

BOOKS BY LUCIEN STRYK

Taproot
The Trespasser
Zen: Poems, Prayers, Sermons, Anecdotes, Interviews
Notes for a Guidebook
Heartland: Poets of the Midwest
World of the Buddha: An Introduction to Buddhist Literature
The Pit and Other Poems
Afterimages: Zen Poems of Shinkichi Takahashi
Twelve Death Poems of the Chinese Zen Masters
Zen Poems of China and Japan: The Crane's Bill
Awakening
Heartland II: Poets of the Midwest
Three Zen Poems
Selected Poems
Haiku of the Japanese Masters
The Duckweed Way: Haiku of Issa
The Penguin Book of Zen Poetry
The Duckpond
Prairie Voices: Poets of Illinois
Zen Poems
Encounter with Zen: Writings on Poetry and Zen
Cherries
Bird of Time: Haiku of Basho
Willows
Collected Poems 1953–1983
On Love and Barley: Haiku of Basho
Triumph of the Sparrow: Zen Poems of Shinkichi Takahashi
Bells of Lombardy
Of Pen and Ink and Paper Scraps
The Dumpling Field: Haiku of Issa

The Gift of Great Poetry

Selected and Introduced by

LUCIEN STRYK

REGNERY GATEWAY *Washington, D.C.*

Publisher's Note: While every effort has been made to acknowledge copyright holders of poems, some copyright holders—despite meticulous research—have been impossible to trace to date.

Due to a lack of space, permissions appear on page 270.

Library of Congress Cataloging-in-Publication Data

The Gift of great poetry / selected and introduced by Lucien Stryk.
p. cm.
ISBN 0-89526-520-6 (cloth ed.)
1. English poetry. 2. American poetry. I. Stryk, Lucien.
PR1175.G46 1992
821.008—dc20 91-44623
CIP

Published in the United States by
Regnery Gateway
1130 17th Street, NW
Washington, DC 20036

Distributed to the trade by
National Book Network
4720-A Boston Way
Lanham, MD 20706

First Edition
Printed on acid free paper
Manufactured in the United States of America

96 95 94 93 92 5 4 3 2 1

To

HELEN

and to

SUZANNE, THEO,

LYDIA, *and* DAN

Contents

INTRODUCTION

1

"You are old, Father William," the young man said,
"And your hair has become very white;
And yet you incessantly stand on your head—
Do you think, at your age, it is right?"

"In my youth," Father William replied to his son,
"I feared it might injure the brain;
But, now that I'm perfectly sure I have none,
Why, I do it again and. . . ."

SUCH AUDACITY, such delightful bantering. It never fails to cart me back, well over half a century, to my first run in with Lewis Carroll. Dawdling home from school, whiffs of mother's cooking coming at me as I round the corner, spur me up the stairs two at a time. Barging in the door, I'm warned by mother not to wake my sister, sleeping in her cot. "Soon as your father gets home," she says when I ask how long until dinner. I turn the radio on to *Jack Armstrong, the All-American Boy*, to be told, "Turn it off before you wake the baby." "What can I do, I'm hungry," I insist. "Go read a book," she says. Somewhat miffed, I go into the living room, screw up a wad of newspaper, kick it across the floor. It lands beneath the bookcase. So I finger spines of books, reluctantly take one from the shelf, sprawl out on the red rug, flip through the pages, begin reading words which suddenly become alive and set me roaring, fit to burst. I read them over, then again, again. "Be off, or I'll kick you downstairs." From that moment on that anthology became important to my life, inspired me when almost twelve years old to write my first poem, *To a Red Rug.*

2

So that is how my first "great" poem affected me. In an age where mediocrity is bloated with hype, raised to heights beyond belief, how to deny the personal element in all such choosing? Yet there are poems written over the last four hundred years that have survived all ravages, seem as fresh today as the moment they were written. I believe the poems in this book are outstanding even among these, have become necessary to those who care for well-made things, and for whom life without great art would be unthinkable. It is one thing to make claims, another to define: what in poetry is greatness?

First, what is a true poem? Ralph Waldo Emerson, master of poetry and prose, described it thus: "It is not meter, but a meter-making argument that makes a poem—a thought so passionate and alive, that, like the spirit of plant or animal, it has an architecture of its own, and adorns nature with a new thing." And the artist capable of writing such a work? He is one with a reserve of sheer intensity, perception, and emotion, who has willed himself to share his vision of the world. And the greatest of all? Here, Thomas Carlyle writes of two such: "Shakespeare does not look at a thing, but into it, through it; so that he constructively comprehends it, can take it asunder and put it together again; the thing melts, as it were, into light under his eye, and anew creates itself before him. That is to say, he is a Poet. For Goethe, as for Shakespeare, the world lies translucent, all fusible we might call it, encircled with wonder; the natural in reality the Supernatural, for to the seer's eyes both become one."

And yet, though we easily name our great poets, it is most difficult to pluck from that deep flow of intensity the finest poems. In all things measurable, scientific discovery, athletic mastery, we tread on safer ground, have few qualms pointing out stellar achievements, but music, painting, poetry? What may be pure gold for one, may prove mere lead to another. Poetry has more in common with painting and music than with other forms of literature. The poet contemplates his work in the same way as composer and painter, hoping to create an object fused with those very elements making up their arts. Poets do not talk, they sing, make pictures. Fine poems and their subjects, material and form, are indivisible, together becoming memorable.

Greatness: how do we know it? Let's begin with the simplest form of awareness. Spine tingles, heart skips, sometimes hair stands on end. A Mozart symphony, a Titian canvas, a Shakespeare monologue will do such things to us, and all of us able to appreciate such works seem to experience them in similar ways. We are transported in the same way every time we see, hear, read a masterwork, and the experience seems greater every time. Such works are inexhaustible, their qualities constant throughout the history of art. In the case of poetry written in English, four hundred years of shifts in taste have not staled the finest of the earlier poems. Here is a stanza from the ancient, anonymous *Tom O' Bedlam's Song*:

> With an host of furious fancies
>   Whereof I am commander,
> With a burning spear and a horse of air
>   To the wilderness I wander.
> By a knight of ghosts and shadows
>   I summoned am to tourney
> Ten leagues beyond the wide world's end,
>   Methinks it is no journey.
>   Yet will I sing: Any food,
>   Any feeding, drink, or clothing?
>   Come, dame or maid, be not afraid,
>   Poor Tom will injure nothing.

Fresh as ever, the poem might have been scribbled this morning. Since encountering Keats's "Eve of St. Agnes," the longest piece in this collection, there has not been a six-month period in which I have not returned to it, and there are other works to which I return avidly. Such joys sustain me, are as essential to me as bread. These poems, of whatever period, share some very basic qualities, chief among them, richness of imagination. In making my choice, I was startled over and over by that richness, finding it as often in lesser known poets, many of whom I passed over through the years, leaping from one high reputation to another. Of equal importance is music, the sonic and metrical appropriateness of what is said. Sound, I discovered long ago, is as much a dimension of meaning as structure, and there are some, a goodly number here, so perfect in music alone that it is virtually possible to dispense with their meaning. Take Walter Savage Landor's *Rose Aylmer*:

> Ah, what avails the sceptered race!
>   Ah, what the form divine!
> What every virtue, every grace!
>   Rose Aylmer, all were thine.
>
> Rose Aylmer, whom these wakeful eyes
>   May weep, but never see,
> A night of memories and sighs
>   I consecrate to thee.

Who could remain unravished by such music? Still, all the elements of good poetry are of a piece, and when its music seems absolute we are all the more likely to respond to its content.

Content, meaning, interest of subject matter very much, with the rare exception of a poem sheerly lyrical, like a cry from the heart. What the poem gives of its maker's vision plays a large role in establishing its worth, assures its life beyond the average span. I choose favorite poets, ultimately, by the amount of life, as we know and experience, they are able to mirror in their works. The range of their emotions matters, I name those great whose visions and insights help me live.

At times, admittedly, their visions may seem overly personal, themes highly complex, and we are forced to throw up our hands. Yet the fact the poet grapples with ideas, pulls fresh thoughts out of the day, makes him exceptional: he has managed somehow to avoid the stupefying entrapments which transform so many into automatons. Indeed a poem offering challenges, as Keats's *Eve of St. Agnes*, may be demanding of the reader's sharp attention, first to the story, simple and straightforward enough, then to the extraordinary flights of imagination, so pungent and colorful. The poet once wrote his contemporary Shelley, for whom he had much admiration, that he might at times stop the breakneck flow of verse to contemplate what he was doing and "load every rift with ore." In no poem of our language is every rift so loaded, and the work is as much a vast canvas, and a symphony, as a poem. Once absorbed as it should be it will prove as permanent for the reader as it is possible for a work of art to be. Keats, who died at 26 years, lived only half as long as Shakespeare and reached heights as dizzying as his.

In our own time and country, Hart Crane, who died young too, reached astonishing levels of intensity, as in this stanza of *Voyages. II*:

> Take this Sea, whose diapason knells
> On scrolls of silver snowy sentences,
> The sceptered terror of whose sessions rends
> As her demeanors motion well or ill,
> All but the pieties of lovers' hands.

The Welshman Dylan Thomas was also doomed to a brief life, but what a life! His poems, which he read to large audiences with an actor's skill, inimitable as they may be, spawned a host of imitators. The poems by Keats, Crane, and Thomas are, to be sure, difficult at first reading, but such poems need to be returned to until they become part of us. It is my conviction that each poem here can be enjoyed; each shares in the imaginative vitality of the whole.

3

It is a mystery, has always been, that no matter how strong the effort, sincere the purpose, however large the gift, an artist cannot will a fine work into being. The poem, as W. B. Yeats puts it, ends with a click, whether begun five years or minutes ago, and until the click is heard there is only a set of words, no more nor less. Indeed nothing can force the satisfactory completion of a work of art. As W. H. Auden said, the true poet differs from the poetaster, from whose fingers poems seem to fly, in that he is never confident that he will write another poem. Yet poets persist, and what makes life endurable is the hope of making something worthwhile. I can imagine no moment as pure, the sort surely Lord Herbert of Cherbury, writing in the 17th century, must have felt when he composed *Elegy Over a Tomb*, the first few stanzas of which go:

Must I then see, alas! eternal night
        Sitting upon those fairest eyes,
And closing all those beams, which once did rise
        So radiant and bright,
That light and heat in them to us did prove
        Knowledge and Love?

Oh, if you did delight no more to stay
        Upon this low and earthly stage,
But rather chose an endless heritage,
        Tell us at least, we pray,
Where all the beauties that those ashes ow'd
        Are now bestow'd?

Doth the Sun now his light with yours renew?
        Have Waves the curling of your hair?
Did you restore unto Sky and Air,
        The red, and white, and blue?
Have you vouchsafed to flow'rs since your death
        That sweetest breath?

In order for a book to become a necessity, to be dipped into when the mood, the need arises, it has to stand, a mansion made of many rooms, all equally essential, however differently appointed. Because the poems herein are arranged chronologically there are, cheek by jowl, pieces vastly different and, necessarily, some startling juxtapositions. Here is a stanza from Lord Byron's *The Sea*:

Roll on, thou deep and dark blue Ocean,—roll!
Ten thousand fleets sweep over thee in vain;
Man marks the earth with ruin,—his control
Stops with the shore;—upon the watery plain
The wrecks are all thy deed, nor doth remain
A shadow of man's ravage, save his own,
When, for a moment, like a drop of rain,
He sinks into thy depths with bubbling groan,
Without a grave, unknelled, uncoffined, and unknown.

And here, from a poem by his contemporary John Clare, *Written in Northampton County Asylum*:

I long for scenes where man has never trod—
For scenes where woman never smiled or wept—
There to abide with my Creator, God,
And sleep as I in childhood sweetly slept,
Full of high thoughts, unborn. So let me lie,—
The grass below; above, the vaulted sky.

The first is part of a sweeping lyric, the second concludes an anguished confession, and the difference between the poems is not one of aesthetics, but character, exposing the nature and being of their makers, one an urbane world-traveling nobleman achieving acclaim and notoriety, the other a peasant for whom poetry, quite suddenly, opened a door to an unimaginable, ultimately destructive world. As to the works, no need to choose: one can move easily, gratefully from one room of the mansion to the other.

Variety is reflected in the choices here. I have been most affected not only by artists capable of covering the full gamut of experience, but by those offering very different moods. How well Shakespeare understood human desire for balance, leavening even the most somber tragedies with scenes of delicious comedy. In most satisfying collections of verse, early to modern, are large, compelling arcs of mood, from dark to light. There is perhaps as much wit as pathos in these pages.

An interesting aspect of these poems is that they reveal so very fully the way succeeding generations have shifted in language use, from the 15th century on, and most dramatically perhaps from the 18th to the 19th. Though we have poets with Latin leanings, like Samuel Johnson, others with Anglo-Saxon, like Jonathan Swift, most, like Shakespeare, have steered a middle course, plucking the finest fruits of both sources, composing as harmoniously as words allow. There are strands, essential, inexpugnable, which stretch throughout, and Shakespeare, among others, assured the permanence of language of his time for the simple reason that our culture could not do without him. In order for us to comprehend him, his very personal use of words, the language must be familiar. In this way it is given fixed form, lastingness, not only in a basic sense but aesthetically. Those who succeeded him and other great poets learned not only the use of words, but their artistic potentials: the stunning metaphor-making of the 17th century, the civilized poise and assurance of the 18th, the rich symbolic flights of the 19th. It has been said that in the arts, present extends the past, is modified by it, and sends it, thus altered, into the future. Which is another way of saying great art is timeless.

4

With only so much space, each poet here, whatever his or her distinction, is represented by one poem. Since I felt obliged to make room for those often bypassed, their works are presented alongside those of the illustrious. So as to represent all periods equally, I have not been able to include many modern works. I felt it to be my task to rescue from obscurity works generally ignored: our verse is so rich and various, all periods so very specially marked, that to focus on "stars," however much their merit, is to give a stunted sense of the whole. Yet there is always bound to be bias of a sort, since editorial tastes differ. Let us take as example Thomas Bailey Aldrich's *Memory*:

> My mind lets go a thousand things,
> Like dates of wars and deaths of kings,
> And yet recalls the very hour—
> 'Twas noon by yonder village tower,
> And on the last blue noon in May—
> The wind came briskly up this way,
> Crisping the brook beside the road;
> Then, pausing here, set down its load
> Of pine-scents, and shook listlessly
> Two petals from that wild-rose tree.

To have survived one hundred years this brief lyric must have pleased even those bred on poetry of large ambition, filled with moral concern and "uplift," a period in which many won distinction for the important things they had to say and for which verse was a convenient vehicle. In the face of all that, as if flaunting its simplicity, this poem gives us virtually the *raison d'etre* of art, our reason for valuing it as much as we do. It is a celebration of the personal, yet makes at the same time, and in the only way art can, a philosophical statement—not through polemic, but imagination. It proclaims what is important as we drift through our life, assaulted by things to which we give passing notice or try vainly to escape. At times when simply forced to close our eyes and ears, turn our backs, suddenly something memorable: two petals falling from a wild-rose tree. How deeply they fall into our lives, momentarily relieving us from harsh reality. Here, in *Leisure*, William Henry Davis, writing closer to our own day, gives us another such moment:

> What is this life if, full of care,
> We have no time to stand and stare.
>
> No time to stand beneath the boughs
> And stare as long as sheep and cows.

I am reminded by these works of those remarkable enlightenment poems written by the Zen Buddhist masters of China and Japan, which for many years now it has been my privilege to translate. Here is one by the Chinese master, Hoin:

On the rocky slope, blossoming
Plums—from where?
Once he saw them, Reiun
Danced all the way to Sandai.

Why are we so well prepared to enjoy such poems? Since the beginning poetry has been based on the qualities they possess, clear structure, arresting imagery, fitting personification, and, always, vital awareness of the particular. We know from their works what was most important to the writers, and what was not. Hence, we know *them*—at least as we find them at these moments of their lives. Something special has been shared, and we are richer. I find myself engaged by works of art in a multitude of ways, sometimes the engagement is lasting, their spirit not only close to but illuminating those things most dear to me. Thus they not only strike home but reveal that what is most valued can be discovered anywhere, any time or place.

5

Years ago in an interview I was asked—in the light of my insistence that art at its best manifests moments of revelation—whether art can accomplish something more, enbrace something larger than the personal. What follows is my response to the interviewer's question, given here for whatever light it may shed and because of the value placed on one of the poems in the collection, William Blake's *London*:

I wander through each chartered street,
Near where the chartered Thames does flow,
And mark in every face I meet
Marks of weakness, marks of woe.

In every cry of every Man,
In every Infant's cry of fear,
In every voice, in every ban,
The mind-forged manacles I hear.

How the chimney-sweeper's cry
Every blackening church appalls;
And the hapless soldier's sigh
Runs in blood down palace walls.

But most through midnight streets I hear
How the youthful harlot's curse
Blasts the new-born infant's tear,
And blights with plagues the marriage hearse.

It extends the imagination: more than anything else it does that. Perhaps the greatest poetry extends and directs it, but all fine poetry does extend, enlarge it. It makes us more than we have been. Really important poetry affects the imagination in a permanent way: it alters it. If we see the imaginative process . . . as being constantly acted upon . . . then those things which touch it have varying results. By some the imagination is substantially affected; by others hardly at all, and, of course, the question is whether the latter are true works of art. . . . You read certain poems . . . a good example might be Blake's *London*.

> It is a short poem that reveals, tremendously, a quality of life. When that happens, art takes on a kind of moral grandeur. What I'm saying . . . is that after reading *London* . . . my view of that time and space is crystallized by the poem. Thus it has historical importance. Whatever London was for Blake, and many others, is given, contained in, that poem. . . . When art can do this, it takes on a dimension that we sometimes forget it is capable of having. But one should not forget.

And yet I would be the first to concede that for every reader moved by *London* there may be some unaffected, perhaps feeling it too harsh and limited a view of so great and various a city. Such readers might very well prefer another view of the city, one filled with glories that give it stature. This, by Blake's contemporary William Wordsworth, is just such a poem about London:

Upon Westminster Bridge

Earth has not anything to show more fair:
Dull would he be of soul who could pass by
A sight so touching in its majesty:
This city now doth like a garment wear
The beauty of the morning; silent, bare,
Ships, towers, domes, theatres and temples lie
Open unto the fields, and to the sky;
All bright and glittering in the smokeless air.
Never did sun more beautifully steep
In his first splendor valley, rock, or hill;
Ne'er saw I, never felt, a calm so deep!

The river glideth at his own sweet will:
Dear God! the very houses seem asleep;
And all that mighty heart is lying still!

Though I have chosen a different Wordsworth poem for this volume, many consider this among his finest. One can accept both London poems as important, yet be aware of the remarkable differences between them. Blake's vision of the city is made up of elements which for a number of reasons might be seen as modern, even "modernist," among them its highly personal imagery. Wordsworth's images, by comparison, are somewhat generic, the sort which might have been found for any great city on a river, with its towers, domes, and theatres. The poet either does not see, or chooses not to, the smoke that has blackened, literally, figuratively, the churches of Blake's London. His is a very attractive personification, with a "mighty heart," whereas Blake's city is placed in one of the lowest circles of hell. It is ironic that while such work won Wordsworth a large, idolatrous audience, Blake, though in later years admired as painter and illustrator, was entirely unknown as poet. Blake died in 1837, and it is only since the mid 1920's that his genius has been acknowledged. Many poets of our time, including W. B. Yeats, who wrote extensively on him, were influenced by Blake, thus paying him the highest form of tribute. Indeed it may not be exaggeration to claim that *The Second Coming*, a poem of startling metaphor, an acknowledged masterwork by which Yeats is represented here, might not have been written as it is, if not for Blake. Here are its final lines:

The darkness drops again; but now I know
That twenty centuries of stony sleep
Were vexed to nightmare by a rocking cradle,
And what rough beast, its hour come round at last,
Slouches towards Bethlehem to be born?

Even as I write I realize the reader may be puzzled, may be wondering, is it the function of a poem to so disturb, are we not sufficiently, daily, assaulted by life's brute facts—poverty, cruelty, violence—without having to face them, magnified, in poetry? Such are the very questions raised and answered by Aristotle in the classic account of aesthetics, *Poetics*. He concedes that though it may be very unpleasant to be confronted with the harsh, something remarkable happens when the art conveying it—drama, painting, poetry—is superior: catharsis. It is a matter of no small importance that through art we are able to live out the most disturbing experiences possible to imagine, and feel as a result unburdened of pain.

But life is not all darkness, there is also *Sweet Content*, as in Thomas Dekker's lyric, the first lines of which go:

Art thou poor, yet hast thou golden slumbers?
O sweet content!
Art thou rich, yet is thy mind perplex'd?
O punishment!
Dost thou laugh to see how fools are vex'd
To add to golden numbers golden numbers?
O sweet content! O sweet, O sweet content!

And who could resist these lines from William Stevenson's rollicking *Jolly Good Ale and Old*:

I cannot eat but little meat,
    My stomach is not good;
But sure I think that I can drink
    With him that wears a hood.
Though I go bare, take ye no care,
    I nothing am a-cold;
I stuff my skin so full within
    Of jolly good ale and old.

6

My hope is that like the poets themselves, whose emotions have been given permanence, the reader's feelings may be mirrored, clarified, even intensified. I go to poems in my need, surrendering to them, for like these poets I am unable to imagine a world without utterance, significant speech. Place a poet in a difficult situation, fetter, chain, torture him, and if in the midst of excruciating pain he finds words to express it, his joy will be boundless. Long after, the true poem made, he will feel all was not in vain. A number of great poems touch on warfare, including one by Wilfrid Owen, who in World War I made the ultimate sacrifice. His war poems, expressive of his noble spirit, will surely bring about a time when war—all wars—will be seen as the maniacal phenomenon poets have named it.

Whether the subject is of light or grave matter, however much the world may benefit, the poet is admired chiefly for his skill in language. Rudyard Kipling explains it in *A Book of Words*:

> The magic of literature lies in words, and not in any man. Witness, a thousand excellent, strenuous words can leave us cold or put us to sleep, whereas a bare half-hundred words breathed upon by some man in his agony, or in his exultation, or in his idleness, ten generations ago, can still lead whole nations into and out of captivity . . . or stir us so intolerably that we can scarcely abide to look at our own souls.

When standing before his countrymen in the ruins of wartime England, so as to rally hearts to even greater sacrifice, Winston Churchill often called upon the poets, quoting stanzas from poems like William Ernest Henley's *Invictus*:

> Out of the night that covers me,
> Black as the pit from pole to pole,
> I thank whatever gods may be
> For my unconquerable soul.
>
> In the fell clutch of circumstance
> I have not winced nor cried aloud.
> Under the bludgeonings of chance
> My head is bloody, but unbow'd.

Rudyard Kipling is correct in claiming that the words by which we choose to live might be "breathed upon by some man in his agony, or in his exultation, or in his idleness. . . ." Yes, even in his idleness. *Delight in Disorder* is my pick of Robert Herrick's lyrics. Here he writes *Upon Julia's Clothes*:

> Whenas in silks my Julia goes,
> Then, then, methinks, how sweetly flows
> The liquefaction of her clothes!
>
> Next, when I cast mine eyes and see
> That brave vibration each way free,
> —O how that glittering taketh me!

I do not think it too much to claim that what has assured a life of well over three hundred years for this poem, and is likely to give it at least as many more, is one word, "liquefaction." It would not of course have such impact in another context, but here the word stirs up music, gathers into itself the "i" sounds in "silks" and "methinks," and sends its "fact" sound into "cast" in the next line and, beyond, in the 5th line into "brave," "ation" and "way." Finally in line 6, its "i" into "glittering" and "a" into "taketh."

There are poems so rich in sound values, such as Gerard Manley Hopkins' *Pied Beauty*, that the words may as well be musical notations. Take the first stanza, which is as much a play on the letter "o" as a celebration of the "pied":

Glory be to God for dappled things—
For skies of couple-colour as a brinded cow;
For rose-moles all in stipple upon trout that swim;
Fresh-firecoal chestnut-falls; finches' wings;
Landscape plotted and pieced—fold, fallow, and plough;
And all trades, their gear and tackle and trim.

At times, as in Wilfrid Owen's *Strange Meeting*, the music achieved by a pronouncedly deliberate device, such as slant rhyme, has a richly organic effect. Here, in the first eight lines, a muffled, dreamlike atmosphere is created, in part by the rhyme:

It seemed that out of battle I escaped
Down some profound dull tunnel, long since scooped
Through granites which titanic wars had groined.
Yet also there encumbered sleepers groaned,
Too fast in thought or death to be bestirred.
Then, as I probed them, one sprang up, and stared
With piteous recognition in fixed eyes,
Lifting distressful hands as if to bless.

That is the way poetry works, and such is the dynamic relationship all words, and their sound, have to each other as they build the poet's vision. If it is true, as claimed, that poets are born, not made, then the best way to identify the truest among them is to look for such signs. The note is unmistakable and is heard throughout the long span of verse in the language. In the case of the finest poets it is heard in their prose, always in

Shakespeare and John Webster, and in Thomas Dekker, author of the blithe *Sweet Content*, who here is found in a mood much more somber (and speaking even to our own time).

Of Winter

> When Charity blows her nails and is ready to starve, yet not so much as a watchman will lend her a flap of his frieze gown to keep her warm: when tradesmen shut up shops, by reason their frozen-hearted creditors go about to nip them with beggary: when the price of sea-coal riseth, and the price of men's labour falleth: when every chimney casts out smoke, but scarce any door opens. . . . when the Thames is covered over with ice and men's hearts caked over and crusted with cruelty: Then mayest thou or any man be bold to swear it is winter.

And here John Donne, who served in the 17th century as Dean of London's St. Paul's Cathedral, in a passage from his 1624 Christmas Eve service:

> He brought light out of darkness, not out of a lesser light; he can bring thy Summer out of Winter, though thou have no Spring; though in the wayes of fortune, or understanding, or conscience, thou have been benighted till now, wintred and frozen, clouded and eclypsed, damped and benummed, smothered and stupefied till now, now God comes to thee, not as

> in the dawning of the day, not as in the bud of the Spring, but as the Sun at noon to illustrate all shadows, as the sheaves in harvest, to fill all penuries, all occasions invite his mercies, and all times are his seasons.

Though John Donne's religious fervor impelled his speech, he must have taken delight, as the never-resting poet in him rose to the moment, in the words themselves. How could he not have? The sublime artist reached once again what for others must have seemed—and in our time still do—unimaginable heights.

7

I consider myself fortunate to have been asked to make a collection of great poems of our language, for to live daily with such works is bracing and ennobling. The task of choosing has been truly daunting: there are so many word masters. I have selected pieces which over many years affected me in most important ways, given me assurance that the art of poetry offers rarest fulfillments. For many poetry not only, as Hamlet puts it to the players, "holds the mirror up to nature, shows virtue her own feature, scorn her own image, and the very age and body of the time his form and pressure," but makes nature, whatever its image, more than bearable—most precious. We are blessed in our language, and the use made of it through the ages by our poets. We owe them our attention, and can best express our gratitude by reading their poems with alert senses, open mind, and receptive spirit.

. . .

My mother is long gone, my father older than Old Father William, my sister caught up in her own life. And I, a father, grandfather, delight even more in:

"You are old, Father William," the young man said,
"And your hair has become very white;
And yet you incessantly stand on your head—
Do you think, at your age, it is right?"

"In my youth," Father William replied to his son,
"I feared it might injure the brain;
But, now that I'm perfectly sure I have none,
Why, I do it again and again."

THE GIFT OF GREAT POETRY

1 ANON

Western Wind

Western wind, when will thou blow,
    The small rain down can rain?
Christ, if my love were in my arms
    And I in my bed again!

2 ANON

Lord Randal

"O where hae ye been, Lord Randal, my son?
O where hae ye been, my handsome young man?"
"I hae been to the wild wood; mother, make my bed soon,
For I'm weary wi hunting, and fain wald lie down."

"Where gat ye your dinner, Lord Randal, my son?
Where gat ye your dinner, my handsome young man?"
"I dined wi my true love; mother, make my bed soon,
For I'm weary wi hunting, and fain wald lie down."

"What gat ye to your dinner, Lord Randal, my son?
What gat ye to your dinner, my handsome young man?"
"I gat eels boiled in broo; mother, make my bed soon,
For I'm weary wi hunting, and fain wald lie down."

"What became of your bloodhounds, Lord Randal, my son?
What became of your bloodhounds, my handsome young man?"
"O they swelld and they died; mother, make my bed soon,
For I'm weary wi hunting, and fain wald lie down."

"O I fear ye are poisond, Lord Randal, my son!
O I fear ye are poisond, my handsome young man!"
"O yes! I am poisond; mother, make my bed soon,
For I'm sick at the heart, and I fain wald lie down."

3 ANON

Sir Patrick Spens

The king sits in Dumferling toune,
  Drinking the blude-reid wine:
O quhar will I get guid sailor,
  To sail this schip of mine?

Up and spak an eldern knicht,
  Sat at the king's richt knee:
Sir Patrick Spens is the best sailor,
  That sails upon the sea.

The king has written a braid letter,
  And signed it wi' his hand;
And sent it to Sir Patrick Spens,
  Was walking on the sand.

The first line that Sir Patrick red,
  A loud lauch lauchèd he:
The next line that Sir Patrick red,
  The teir blinded his ee.

O quhar is this has don this deid,
  This ill deid don to me;
To send me out this time o' the yeir,
  To sail upon the sea?

Mak haste, mak haste, my mirry men all,
  Our good schip sails the morn.

O say na sae, my master deir,
For I feir a deadlie storme.

Late late yestreen I saw the new moone
Wi' the auld moone in hir arme;
And I feir, I feir, my deir master,
That we will come to harme.

O our Scots nobles wer richt laith
To weet their cork-heild schoone;
But lang owre a' the play were played,
Their hats they swam aboone.

O lang, lang may the ladies stand
Wi' their fans into their hand,
Or e'er they see Sir Patrick Spens
Come sailing to the land.

O lang, lang, may the ladies stand
Wi' their gold kems in their hair,
Waiting for their ain deir lords,
For they'll see them na mair.

Have owre, have owre to Aberdour,
It's fifty fadom deip:
And thair lies guid Sir Patrick Spens,
Wi' the Scots lords at his feit.

4 ANON

Edward, Edward

'Why does your brand sae drop wi' blude,
Edward, Edward?
Why does your brand sae drop wi' blude,
And why sae sad gang ye, O?'
'O I hae kill'd my hawk sae gude,
Mither, mither;
O I hae kill'd my hawk sae gude,
And I had nae mair but he, O.'

'Your hawk's blude was never sae red,
Edward, Edward;
Your hawk's blude was never sae red,
My dear son, I tell thee, O.'
'O I hae kill'd my red-roan steed,
Mither, mither;
O I hae kill'd my red-roan steed,
That erst was sae fair and free, O.'

'Your steed was auld, and ye hae got mair;
Edward, Edward;
Your steed was auld, and ye hae got mair;
Some other dule ye dree, O.'
'O I hae kill'd my father dear,
Mither, mither;
O I hae kill'd my father dear,
Alas, and wae is me, O!'

'And whatten penance will ye dree for that,
        Edward, Edward?
Whatten penance will ye dree for that?
    My dear son, now tell me, O.'
'I'll set my feet in yonder boat,
        Mither, mither;
I'll set my feet in yonder boat,
    And I'll fare over the sea, O.'

'And what will ye do wi' your tow'rs and your ha',
        Edward, Edward?
And what will ye do wi' your tow'rs and your ha',
    That were sae fair to see, O?'
'I'll let them stand till they doun fa',
        Mither, mither;
I'll let them stand till they doun fa',
    For here never mair maun I be, O.'

'And what will ye leave to your bairns and your wife,
        Edward, Edward?
And what will ye leave to your bairns and your wife,
    When ye gang owre the sea, O?'
'The warld's room: let them beg through life,
        Mither, mither;
The warld's room: let them beg through life;
    For them never mair will I see, O.'

'And what will ye leave to your ain mither dear,
        Edward, Edward?
And what will ye leave to your ain mither dear,
    My dear son, now tell me, O?'

'The curse of hell frae me sall ye bear,
Mither, mither,
The curse of hell frae me sall ye bear:
Sic counsels ye gave to me, O!'

5 ANON

Bonny Barbara Allan

It was in and about the Martinmas time,
  When the green leaves were a falling,
That Sir John Graeme, in the West Country,
  Fell in love with Barbara Allan.

He sent his man down through the town,
  To the place where she was dwelling:
"O haste and come to my master dear,
  Gin ye be Barbara Allan."

O hooly, hooly rose she up,
  To the place where he was lying,
And when she drew the curtain by,
  "Young man, I think you're dying."

"O it's I'm sick, and very, very sick,
  And 'tis a' for Barbara Allan;"
"O the better for me ye's never be,
  Tho your heart's blood were a spilling."

"O dinna ye mind, young man," said she,
  "When ye was in the tavern a drinking,
That ye made the healths gae round and round,
  And slighted Barbara Allan?"

He turned his face unto the wall,
  And death was with him dealing:

"Adieu, adieu, my dear friends all,
  And be kind to Barbara Allan."

And slowly, slowly raise she up,
  And slowly, slowly left him,
And sighing said, she could not stay,
  Since death of life had reft him.

She had not gane a mile but twa,
  When she heard the dead-bell ringing,
And every jow that the dead-bell geid,
  It cry'd, Woe to Barbara Allan!

"O Mother, mother, make my bed!
  O make it saft and narrow!
Since my love died for me to-day,
  I'll die for him to-morrow."

6 ANON

Beware Fair Maid

Beware fair maid of musky courtiers' oaths,
Take heed what gifts and favors you receive,
Let not the fading gloss of silken clothes
Dazzle your virtue, or your fame bereave.
  For lose but once the hold you have of grace,
  Who'll e'er respect your fortune or your face?

Each greedy hand will strive to catch the flower
When none regards the stalk it grows upon,
Each creature seeks the fruit still to devour
But leave the tree to fall or stand alone.
  Yet this advice, fair creature, take of me,
  Let none take fruit, unless he take the tree.

Believe no oaths, nor much protesting men,
Credit no vows, nor no bewailing songs,
Let courtiers swear, forswear, and swear again;
Their hearts do live ten regions from their tongues.
  For when with oaths they make thy heart to tremble
  Believe them least, for then they most dissemble.

Beware lest Caesar do corrupt thy mind
Or fond Ambition sell thy modesty.
Say though a king thou ever courteous find
He cannot garden thy virginity.
  Begin with king, to subject you will fall,
  From lord to lackey, and at last to all.

7 ANON

Tom O' Bedlam's Song

From the hag and hungry goblin
  That into rags would rend ye,
And the spirit that stands by the naked man
  In the book of moons, defend ye,
That of your five sound senses
  You never be forsaken,
Nor wander from yourselves with Tom,
  Abroad to beg your bacon.
    While I do sing: Any food,
      Any feeding, drink, or clothing?
    Come, dame or maid, be not afraid,
      Poor Tom will injure nothing.

Of thirty bare years have I
  Twice twenty been enragèd,
And of forty been three times fifteen
  In durance soundly cagèd
On the lordly lofts of Bedlam,
  With stubble soft and dainty,
Brave bracelets strong, sweet whips, ding-dong,
  With wholesome hunger plenty.
    And now I sing: Any food,
      Any feeding, drink, or clothing?
    Come, dame or maid, be not afraid,
      Poor Tom will injure nothing.

With a thought I took for Maudlin,
  And a cruse of cockle pottage,

With a thing thus tall, sky bless you all,
  I befell into this dotage.
I slept not since the Conquest,
  Till then I never wakèd,
Till the roguish boy of love where I lay
  Me found and stripped me naked.
    And now I sing: Any food,
      Any feeding, drink, or clothing?
    Come, dame or maid, be not afraid,
      Poor Tom will injure nothing.

When I short have shorn my sour-face,
  And swigged my horny barrel,
In an oaken inn I pound my skin,
  As a suit of gilt apparel.
The moon's my constant mistress,
  And the lowly owl my morrow;
The flaming drake and the night-crow make
  Me music to my sorrow.
    While I do sing: Any food,
      Any feeding, drink, or clothing?
    Come, dame or maid, be not afraid,
      Poor Tom will injure nothing.

The palsy plagues my pulses,
  When I prig your pigs or pullen,
Your culvers take, or matchless make
  Your chanticleer or sullen.
When I want provant, with Humphry
  I sup, and when benighted,
I repose in Powles with waking souls,

Yet never am affrighted.
But I do sing: Any food,
Any feeding, drink, or clothing?
Come, dame or maid, be not afraid,
Poor Tom will injure nothing.

I know more than Apollo,
For oft when he lies sleeping,
I see the stars at bloody wars
In the wounded welkin weeping,
The moon embrace her shepherd,
And the queen of love her warrior,
While the first doth horn the star of morn,
And the next the heavenly Farrier.
While I do sing: Any food,
Any feeding, drink, or clothing?
Come, dame or maid, be not afraid,
Poor Tom will injure nothing.

The gipsy Snap and Pedro
Are none of Tom's comradoes.
The punk I scorn, and the cutpurse sworn,
And the roaring boys' bravadoes.
The meek, the white, the gentle,
Me handle, touch, and spare not;
But those that cross Tom Rhinoceros
Do what the panther dare not.
Although I sing: Any food,
Any feeding, drink, or clothing?
Come, dame or maid, be not afraid,
Poor Tom will injure nothing.

With an host of furious fancies
  Whereof I am commander,
With a burning spear and a horse of air
  To the wilderness I wander.
By a knight of ghosts and shadows
  I summoned am to tourney
Ten leagues beyond the wide world's end,
  Methinks it is no journey.
    Yet will I sing: Any food,
      Any feeding, drink, or clothing?
    Come, dame or maid, be not afraid,
      Poor Tom will injure nothing.

8 ANON

The Vicar of Bray

In good King Charles's golden days,
  When loyalty no harm meant,
A zealous high-churchman was I,
  And so I got preferment.
To teach my flock I never missed:
  Kings were by God appointed,
And lost are those that dare resist
  Or touch the Lord's anointed.
    And this is law that I'll maintain
      Until my dying day, sir,
    That whatsoever king shall reign,
      Still I'll be the Vicar of Bray, sir.

When royal James possessed the crown,
  And popery came in fashion,
The penal laws I hooted down,
  And read the Declaration;
The Church of Rome I found would fit
  Full well my constitution;
And I had been a Jesuit
  But for the Revolution.
    And this is law, etc.

When William was our king declared,
  To ease the nation's grievance;
With this new wind about I steered,
  And swore to him allegiance;

Old principles I did revoke,
  Set conscience at a distance;
Passive obedience was a joke,
  A jest was non-resistance.
    And this is law, etc.

When royal Anne became our queen,
  The Church of England's glory,
Another face of things was seen,
  And I became a Tory;
Occasional conformists base,
  I blamed their moderation;
And thought the Church in danger was,
  By such prevarication.
    And this is law, etc.

When George in pudding-time came o'er,
  And moderate men looked big, sir,
My principles I changed once more,
  And so became a Whig, sir;
And thus preferment I procured
  From our new faith's-defender,
And almost every day abjured
  The Pope and the Pretender.
    And this is law, etc.

The illustrious house of Hanover,
  And Protestant succession,
To these I do allegiance swear—
  While they can keep possession:
For in my faith and loyalty

I nevermore will falter,
And George my lawful king shall be—
Until the times do alter.
And this is law, etc.

9 JOHN SKELTON

To Mistress Margaret Hussey

Merry Margaret
As midsummer flower,
Gentle as falcon
Or hawk of the tower:
With solace and gladness,
Much mirth and no madness,
All good and no badness;
So joyously,
So maidenly,
So womanly
Her demeaning
In every thing,
Far, far passing
That I can indite,
Or suffice to write
Of Merry Margaret
As midsummer flower
Gentle as falcon
Or hawk of the tower.
As patient and still
And as full of good will
As fair Isaphill,
Coliander,
Sweet pomander,
Good Cassander;
Steadfast of thought,
Well made, well wrought,

Far may be sought,
Ere that ye can find
So courteous, so kind
As merry Margaret,
This midsummer flower,
Gentle as falcon
Or hawk of the tower.

10 SIR THOMAS WYATT

They Flee From Me

They flee from me that sometime did me seek,
With naked foot stalking in my chamber:
I have seen them gentle, tame, and meek,
That now are wild, and do not once remember
That sometime they have put themselves in danger
To take bread at my hand; and now they range,
Busily seeking with a continual change.

Thanked be fortune, it hath been otherwise
Twenty times better; but once, in special,
In thin array, after a pleasant guise,
When her loose gown from her shoulders did fall,
And she me caught in her arms long and small,
Therewith all sweetly did me kiss,
And softly said, '*Dear heart, how like you this?*'

It was no dream; I lay broad waking:
But all is turned, thorough my gentleness,
Into a strange fashion of forsaking;
And I have leave to go, of her goodness;
And she also to use new-fangleness.
But since that I so unkindely am served,
I fain would know what she hath deserved.

11 HENRY HOWARD, EARL OF SURREY

Give Place, Ye Lovers, Here Before

Give place, ye lovers, here before
That spent your boasts and brags in vain;
My lady's beauty passeth more
The best of yours, I dare well sayn
Than doth the sun the candlelight,
Or brightest day the darkest night,

And thereto hath a troth as just
As had Penelope the fair,
For what she saith, ye may it trust
As it by writing sealéd were,
And virtues hath she many moe
Than I with pen have skill to show.

I could rehearse, if that I wold,
The whole effect of Nature's plaint,
When she had lost the perfect mold
The like to whom she could not paint;
With wringing hands how she did cry
And what she said, I know it, I.

I know she swore, with raging mind,
Her kingdom only set apart,
There was no loss, by law of kind,
That could have gone so near her heart;

And this was chiefly all her pain:
She could not make the like again.

Sith nature thus gave her the praise
To be the chiefest work she wrought,
In faith, methinks some better ways
On your behalf might well be sought
Than to compare, as ye have done,
To match the candle with the sun.

12 WILLIAM STEVENSON

Jolly Good Ale and Old

I cannot eat but little meat,
My stomach is not good;
But sure I think that I can drink
With him that wears a hood.
Though I go bare, take ye no care,
I nothing am a-cold;
I stuff my skin so full within
Of jolly good ale and old.
Back and side go bare, go bare;
Both foot and hand go cold;
But, belly, God send thee good ale enough,
Whether it be new or old.

I love no roast but a nut-brown toast,
And a crab laid in the fire;
A little bread shall do me stead;
Much bread I not desire.
No frost nor snow, no wind, I trow,
Can hurt me if I wold;
I am so wrapp'd and thoroughly lapp'd
Of jolly good ale and old.
Back and side go bare, go bare, &c.

And Tib, my wife, that as her life
Loveth well good ale to seek,
Full oft drinks she till ye may see
The tears run down her cheek:

Then doth she trowl to me the bowl
  Even as a maltworm should,
And saith, 'Sweetheart, I took my part
  Of this jolly good ale and old.'
    Back and side go bare, go bare, &c.

Now let them drink till they nod and wink,
  Even as good fellows should do;
They shall not miss to have that bliss
  Good ale doth bring men to;
And all poor souls that have scour'd bowls
  Or have them lustily troll'd,
God save the lives of them and their wives,
  Whether they be young or old.
    Back and side go bare, go bare;
    Both foot and hand go cold;
    But, belly, God send thee good ale enough,
    Whether it be new or old.

13 SIR EDWARD DYER

My Mind to Me a Kingdom Is

My mind to me a kingdom is,
  Such present joys therein I find,
That it excels all other bliss
  That earth affords or grows by kind:
Though much I want which most would have,
Yet still my mind forbids to crave.

No princely pomp, no wealthy store,
  No force to win the victory,
No wily wit to salve a sore,
  No shape to feed a loving eye;
To none of these I yield as thrall:
For why? My mind doth serve for all.

I see how plenty [surfeits] oft,
  And hasty climbers soon do fall;
I see that those which are aloft
  Mishap doth threaten most of all;
They get with toil, they keep with fear:
Such cares my mind could never bear.

Content to live, this is my stay;
  I seek no more than may suffice;
I press to bear no haughty sway;
  Look, what I lack my mind supplies:
Lo, thus I triumph like a king,
Content with that my mind doth bring.

Some have too much, yet still do crave;
  I little have, and seek no more.
They are but poor, though much they have,
  And I am rich with little store;
They poor, I rich; they beg, I give;
They lack, I leave; they pine, I live.

I laugh not at another's loss;
  I grudge not at another's gain;
No worldly waves my mind can toss;
  My state at one doth still remain:
I fear no foe, I fawn no friend;
I loathe not life, nor dread my end.

Some weigh their pleasure by their lust,
  Their wisdom by their rage of will;
Their treasure is their only trust;
  A cloakèd craft their store of skill:
But all the pleasure that I find
Is to maintain a quiet mind.

My wealth is health and perfect ease;
  My conscience clear my chief defense;
I neither seek by bribes to please,
  Nor by deceit to breed offense:
Thus do I live; thus will I die;
Would all did so as well as I!

14 EDWARD DE VERE, EARL OF OXFORD

Epigram

Were I a king, I could command content;
Were I obscure, hidden should be my cares;
Or were I dead, no cares should me torment,
No hopes, no hates, nor loves, nor griefs, nor fears.
A doubtful choice, of these three which to crave—
A kingdom, or a cottage, or a grave.

15 SIR WALTER RALEIGH

His Pilgrimage

Give me my scallop-shell of quiet,
My staff of faith to walk upon,
My scrip of joy, immortal diet,
My bottle of salvation,
My gown of glory, hope's true gage;
And thus I'll take my pilgrimage.

Blood must be my body's balmer;
No other balm will there be given;
Whilst my soul, like quiet palmer,
Travelleth towards the land of heaven;
Over the silver mountains,
Where spring the nectar fountains;
There will I kiss
The bowl of bliss;
And drink mine everlasting fill
Upon every milken hill.
My soul will be a-dry before;
But, after, it will thirst no more.

16 EDMUND SPENSER

Unhappy Verse

Unhappy Verse, the witnesse of my unhappie state,
Make thy selfe fluttring wings of thy fast flying
Thought, and fly forth unto my Love, whersoever she be:
Whether lying reastlesse in heavy bed, or else
Sitting so cheerelesse at the cheerfull boord, or else
Playing alone carelesse on her heavenlie Virginals.
If in Bed, tell her that my eyes can take no rest;
If at Boord, tell her that my mouth can eat no meate;
If at her Virginals, tell her I can heare no mirth.
Asked why? say, Waking Love suffereth no sleepe;
Say that raging Love doth appall the weak stomacke;
Say that lamenting Love marreth the Musicall.
Tell her that her pleasures were wonte to lull me asleepe;
Tell her that her beautie was wonte to feede mine eyes;
Tell her that her sweete Tongue was wont to make me
mirth.
Nowe do I nightly waste, wanting my kindely rest;
Nowe do I dayly starve, wanting my lively food?
Nowe do I alwayes dye, wanting thy timely mirth.
And if I waste, who will bewaile my heavy chaunce?
And if I starve, who will record my cursed end?
And if I dye, who will saye, *this was Immerito?*

17 SIR PHILIP SIDNEY

FROM *Astrophel and Stella*

Loving in truth, and faine in verse my love to show,
That she (deare she) might take some pleasure of my paine:
Pleasure might cause her reade, reading might make her know,
Knowledge might pitie winne, and pitie grace obtaine,
I sought fit words to paint the blackest face of woe,
Studying inventions fine, her wits to entertaine:
Oft turning others leaves, to see if thence would flow
Some fresh and fruitfull showers upon my sunne-burn'd braine.

But words came halting forth, wanting Inventions stay,
Invention Natures child, fled step-dame Studies blowes,
And others feete still seem'd but strangers in my way.
Thus great with child to speake, and helplesse in my throwes
Biting my trewand pen, beating my selfe for spite,
Foole, said my Muse to me, looke in thy heart and write.

18 GEORGE PEELE

The Voice from the Well

Gently dip: but not too deepe;
For feare you make the goulden beard to weepe.
Faire maiden white and red,
Combe me smoothe, and stroke my head:
And thou shalt have some cockell bread.
Gently dippe, but not too deepe,
For feare thou make the goulden beard to weep.
Faire maide, white, and redde,
Combe me smooth, and stroke my head;
And every haire, a sheave shall be,
And every sheave a goulden tree.

19 THOMAS LODGE

Rosalind's Madrigal

Love in my bosom like a bee
        Doth suck his sweet:
Now with his wings he plays with me,
        Now with his feet.
Within mine eyes he makes his nest,
His bed amidst my tender breast;
My kisses are his daily feast,
And yet he robs me of my rest:
        Ah! wanton, will ye?

And if I sleep, then percheth he
        With pretty flight,
And makes his pillow of my knee
        The livelong night.
Strike I my lute, he tunes the string;
He music plays if so I sing;
He lends me every lovely thing,
Yet cruel he my heart doth sting:
        Whist, wanton, still ye!

Else I with roses every day
        Will whip you hence,
And bind you, when you long to play,
        For your offence.
I'll shut mine eyes to keep you in;
I'll make you fast it for your sin;
I'll count your power not worth a pin.

—Alas! what hereby shall I win
        If he gainsay me?

What if I beat the wanton boy
        With many a rod?
He will repay me with annoy,
        Because a god.
Then sit thou safely on my knee;
Then let thy bower my bosom be;
Lurk in mine eyes, I like of thee;
O Cupid, so thou pity me,
        Spare not, but play thee!

20 CHRISTOPHER MARLOWE

The Passionate Shepherd to His Love

Come live with me and be my Love,
And we will all the pleasures prove
That hills and valleys, dales and fields,
Or woods or steepy mountain yields.

And we will sit upon the rocks,
And see the shepherds feed their flocks
By shallow rivers, to whose falls
Melodious birds sing madrigals.

And I will make thee beds of roses
And a thousand fragrant posies;
A cap of flowers, and a kirtle
Embroider'd all with leaves of myrtle.

A gown made of the finest wool
Which from our pretty lambs we pull;
Fair-linèd slippers for the cold,
With buckles of the purest gold.

A belt of straw and ivy-buds
With coral clasps and amber studs:
And if these pleasures may thee move,
Come live with me and be my Love.

The shepherd swains shall dance and sing
For thy delight each May morning:

If these delights thy mind may move,
Then live with me and be my Love.

Her Reply

(WRITTEN BY SIR WALTER RALEIGH)

If all the world and love were young,
And truth in every shepherd's tongue,
These pretty pleasures might me move
To live with thee and be thy Love.

But Time drives flocks from field to fold;
When rivers rage and rocks grow cold;
And Philomel becometh dumb;
The rest complains of cares to come.

The flowers do fade, and wanton fields
To wayward Winter reckoning yields:
A honey tongue, a heart of gall,
Is fancy's spring, but sorrow's fall.

Thy gowns, thy shoes, thy beds of roses,
Thy cap, thy kirtle, and thy posies,
Soon break, soon wither—soon forgotten,
In folly ripe, in reason rotten.

Thy belt of straw and ivy-buds,
Thy coral clasps and amber studs,—

All these in me no means can move
To come to thee and be thy Love.

But could youth last, and love still breed,
Had joys no date, nor age no need,
Then these delights my mind might move
To live with thee and be thy Love.

21 WILLIAM SHAKESPEARE

Let Me Not

Let me not to the marriage of true minds
Admit impediments. Love is not love
Which alters when it alteration finds,
Or bends with the remover to remove:
O, no! it is an ever-fixèd mark,
That looks on tempests and is never shaken;
It is the star to every wand'ring bark,
Whose worth's unknown, although his height be taken.
Love's not Time's fool, though rosy lips and cheeks
Within his bending sickle's compass come;
Love alters not with his brief hours and weeks,
But bears it out even to the edge of doom:—
    If this be error and upon me proved,
    I never writ, nor no man ever loved.

22 THOMAS CAMPION

Cherry-Ripe

There is a garden in her face
  Where roses and white lilies blow;
A heavenly paradise is that place,
  Wherein all pleasant fruits do flow;
There cherries grow that none may buy
Till "Cherry-Ripe" themselves do cry.

Those cherries fairly do enclose
  Of orient pearl, a double row,
Which when her lovely laughter shows,
  They look like rose-buds fill'd with snow;
Yet them nor peer nor prince may buy,
Till "Cherry-Ripe" themselves do cry.

Her eyes like angels watch them still;
  Her brows like bended bows do stand,
Threat'ning with piercing frowns to kill
  All that attempt with eye or hand
These sacred cherries to come nigh,
Till "Cherry-Ripe" themselves do cry!

23 THOMAS NASHE

Song

Adieu, farewell earths blisse,
This world uncertaine is,
Fond are lifes lustfull joyes,
Death proves them all but toyes,
None from his darts can flye,
I am sick, I must dye:
        Lord have mercy on us.

Rich men, trust not in wealth,
Gold cannot buy you health,
Phisick himselfe must fade.
All things, to end are made,
The plague full swift goes bye,
I am sick, I must dye:
        Lord have mercy on us.

Beauty is but a flowre,
Which wrinckles will devoure,
Brightness falls from the ayre,
Queenes have died yong, and faire,
Dust hath closde *Helens* eye.
I am sick, I must dye:
        Lord have mercy on us.

Strength stoopes unto the grave,
Wormes feed on *Hector* brave,
Swords may not fight with fate,

Earth still holds ope her gate.
Come, come, the bells do crye.
I am sick, I must dye:
        Lord have mercy on us.

Wit with his wantonesse,
Tasteth deaths bitterness:
Hels executioner,
Hath no eares for to heare
What vaine art can reply.
I am sick, I must dye:
        Lord have mercy on us.

Haste therefore eche degree,
To welcome destiny:
Heaven is our heritage,
Earth but a players stage,
Mount wee unto the sky.
I am sick, I must dye:
        Lord have mercy on us.

24 SIR HENRY WOTTON

Upon the Death of Sir Albert Morton's Wife

He first deceased; she for a little tried
To live without him, liked it not, and died.

25 BEN JONSON

To Celia

Drink to me only with thine eyes,
    And I will pledge with mine;
Or leave a kiss but in the cup
    And I'll not look for wine.
The thirst that from the soul doth rise
    Doth ask a drink divine;
But might I of Jove's nectar sup,
    I would not change for thine.

I sent thee late a rosy wreath,
    Not so much honouring thee
As giving it a hope that there
    It could not wither'd be;
But thou thereon didst only breathe,
    And sent'st it back to me;
Since when it grows, and smells, I swear,
    Not of itself but thee!

26 JOHN DONNE

Song

Go and catch a falling star,
  Get with child a mandrake root,
Tell me where all past years are,
  Or who cleft the Devil's foot;
Teach me to hear mermaids singing,
Or to keep off envy's stinging,
    And find
    What wind
Serves to advance an honest mind.

If thou be'st born to strange sights,
  Things invisible to see,
Ride ten thousand days and nights
  Till Age snow white hairs on thee;
Thou, when thou return'st, wilt tell me
All strange wonders that befell thee,
    And swear
    No where
Lives a woman true and fair.

If thou find'st one, let me know;
  Such a pilgrimage were sweet.
Yet do not; I would not go,
  Though at next door we might meet.

Though she were true when you met her,
And last till you write your letter,
            Yet she
            Will be
False, ere I come, to two or three.

27 THOMAS DEKKER

Sweet Content

Art thou poor, yet hast thou golden slumbers?
O sweet content!
Art thou rich, yet is thy mind perplex'd?
O punishment!
Dost thou laugh to see how fools are vex'd
To add to golden numbers golden numbers?
O sweet content! O sweet, O sweet content!
Work apace, apace, apace, apace;
Honest labour bears a lovely face;
Then hey nonny nonny—hey nonny nonny!

Canst drink the waters of the crispèd spring?
O sweet content!
Swim'st thou in wealth, yet sink'st in thine own tears?
O punishment!
Then he that patiently want's burden bears,
No burden bears, but is a king, a king!
O sweet content! O sweet, O sweet content!
Work apace, apace, apace, apace;
Honest labour bears a lovely face;
Then hey nonny nonny—hey nonny nonny!

28 JOHN WEBSTER

A Dirge

Call for the robin-redbreast and the wren,
Since o'er shady groves they hover,
And with leaves and flowers do cover
The friendless bodies of unburied men.
Call unto his funeral dole
The ant, the field-mouse, and the mole,
To rear him hillocks that shall keep him warm,
And (when gay tombs are robb'd) sustain no harm;
But keep the wolf far thence, that's foe to men,
For with his nails he'll dig them up again.

29 LORD HERBERT OF CHERBURY

Elegy over a Tomb

Must I then see, alas! eternal night
Sitting upon those fairest eyes,
And closing all those beams, which once did rise
So radiant and bright,
That light and heat in them to us did prove
Knowledge and Love?

Oh, if you did delight no more to stay
Upon this low and earthly stage,
But rather chose an endless heritage,
Tell us at least, we pray,
Where all the beauties that those ashes ow'd
Are now bestow'd?

Doth the Sun now his light with yours renew?
Have Waves the curling of your hair?
Did you restore unto the Sky and Air,
The red, and white, and blue?
Have you vouchsafed to flow'rs since your death
That sweetest breath?

Had not Heav'ns Lights else in their houses slept,
Or to some private life retir'd?
Must not the Sky and Air have else conspir'd?
And in their Regions wept?
Must not each flower else the earth could breed
Have been a weed?

But thus enrich'd may we not yield some cause
Why they themselves lament no more?
That must have changed the course they held before,
And broke their proper Laws,
Had not your beauties giv'n this second birth
To Heaven and Earth?

Tell us—for Oracles must still ascend,
For those that crave them at your tomb—
Tell us, where are those beauties now become,
And what they now intend:
Tell us, alas, that cannot tell our grief,
Or hope relief.

30 ROBERT HERRICK

Delight in Disorder

A sweet disorder in the dress
Kindles in clothes a wantonness:
A lawn about the shoulders thrown
Into a fine distraction:
An erring lace, which here and there
Enthrals the crimson stomacher:
A cuff neglectful, and thereby
Ribbands to flow confusedly:
A winning wave, deserving note,
In the tempestuous petticoat:
A careless shoe-string, in whose tie
I see a wild civility:
Do more bewitch me than when art
Is too precise in every part.

31 GEORGE HERBERT

Love

Love bade me welcome; yet my soul drew back,
 Guilty of dust and sin.
But quick-eyed Love, observing me grow slack
 From my first entrance in,
Drew nearer to me, sweetly questioning
 If I lack'd anything.

'A guest,' I answer'd, 'worthy to be here:'
 Love said, 'You shall be he.'
'I, the unkind, ungrateful? Ah, my dear,
 I cannot look on Thee.'
Love took my hand and smiling did reply,
 'Who made the eyes but I?'

'Truth, Lord; but I have marr'd them: let my shame
 Go where it doth deserve.'
'And know you not,' says Love, 'Who bore the blame?'
 'My dear, then I will serve.'
'You must sit down,' says Love, 'and taste my meat.'
 So I did sit and eat.

32 THOMAS CAREW

A Song

Ask me no more where Jove bestows,
When June is past, the fading rose;
For in your beauty's orient deep
These flowers, as in their causes, sleep.

Ask me no more whither doth stray
The golden atoms of the day;
For in pure love heaven did prepare
Those powders to enrich your hair.

Ask me no more whither doth haste
The nightingale when May is past;
For in your sweet dividing throat
She winters, and keeps warm her note.

Ask me no more where those stars light
That downwards fall in dead of night;
For in your eyes they sit, and there
Fixèd become as in their sphere.

Ask me no more if east or west
The phoenix builds her spicy nest;
For unto you at last she flies,
And in your fragrant bosom dies.

33 JAMES SHIRLEY

Death the Leveller

The glories of our blood and state
Are shadows, not substantial things;
There is no armour against Fate;
    Death lays his icy hand on kings:
            Sceptre and Crown
            Must tumble down,
And in the dust be equal made
With the poor crookèd scythe and spade.

Some men with swords may reap the field,
    And plant fresh laurels where they kill:
But their strong nerves at last must yield;
    They tame but one another still:
            Early or late
            They stoop to fate,
And must give up their murmuring breath
When they, pale captives, creep to death.

The garlands wither on your brow;
    Then boast no more your mighty deeds!
Upon Death's purple altar now
    See where the victor-victim bleeds.
            Your heads must come
            To the cold tomb:
Only the actions of the just
Smell sweet and blossom in their dust.

34 WILLIAM STRODE

On Westwall Downes

When Westwall Downes I gan to tread,
Where cleanely wynds the greene did sweepe,
Methought a landskipp there was spread,
Here a bush and there a sheepe:
    The pleated wrinkles of the face
    Of wave-swolne earth did lend such grace,
    As shadowings in Imag'ry
    Which both deceive and please the eye.

The sheepe sometymes did tread the maze
By often wynding in and in,
And sometymes round about they trace
Which mylkmaydes call a Fairie ring:
    Such semicircles have they runne,
    Such lynes across so trymly spunne
    That sheppeards learne whenere they please
    A new Geometry with ease.

The slender food upon the downe
Is allwayes even, allwayes bare,
Which neither spring nor winter's frowne
Can ought improve or ought impayre:
    Such is the barren Eunuches chynne,
    Which thus doth evermore begynne
With tender downe to be orecast
    Which never comes to haire at last.

Here and there twoe hilly crests
Amiddst them hugg a pleasant greene,
And these are like twoe swelling breasts
That close a tender fall betweene.
    Here would I sleepe, or read, or pray
    From early morn till flight of day:
    But harke! a sheepe-bell calls mee upp,
    Like Oxford colledge bells, to supp.

35 EDMUND WALLER

Go, Lovely Rose

Go, lovely Rose—
Tell her that wastes her time and me,
That now she knows,
When I resemble her to thee,
How sweet and fair she seems to be.

Tell her that's young,
And shuns to have her graces spied,
That hadst thou sprung
In deserts where no men abide,
Thou must have uncommended died.

Small is the worth
Of beauty from the light retired:
Bid her come forth,
Suffer herself to be desired,
And not blush so to be admired.

Then die—that she
The common fate of all things rare
May read in thee;
How small a part of time they share
That are so wondrous sweet and fair!

36 JOHN MILTON

On His Blindness

When I consider how my light is spent,
E're half my days, in this dark world and wide,
And that one Talent which is death to hide,
Lodg'd with me useless, though my Soul more bent
To serve therewith my Maker, and present
My true account, least he returning chide,
Doth God exact day-labour, light deny'd,
I fondly ask; But patience to prevent
That murmur, soon replies, God doth not need
Either man's work or his own gifts, who best
Bear his milde yoak, they serve him best, his State
Is Kingly. Thousands at his bidding speed
And post o're Land and Ocean without rest:
They also serve who only stand and waite.

37 SIR JOHN SUCKLING

The Constant Lover

Out upon it, I have loved
  Three whole days together!
And am like to love three more,
  If it prove fair weather.

Time shall moult away his wings
  Ere he shall discover
In the whole wide world again
  Such a constant lover.

But the spite on 't is, no praise
  Is due at all to me:
Love with me had made no stays,
  Had it any been but she.

Had it any been but she,
  And that very face,
There had been at least ere this
  A dozen dozen in her place.

To Chloe

Who for his sake wished herself younger

There are two births; the one when light
  First strikes the new awaken'd sense;
The other when two souls unite,
  And we must count our life from thence:
When you loved me and I loved you
Then both of us were born anew.

Love then to us new souls did give
  And in those souls did plant new powers;
Since when another life we live,
  The breath we breathe is his, not ours:
Love makes those young whom age doth chill,
And whom he finds young keeps young still.

39 THOMAS JORDAN

Let Us Drink

Let us drink and be merry, dance, joke, and rejoice,
With claret and sherry, theorbo and voice!
The changeable world to our joy is unjust,
All treasure's uncertain,
Then down with your dust!
In frolics dispose your pounds, shillings, and pence,
For we shall be nothing a hundred years hence.

We'll sport and be free with Moll, Betty, and Dolly,
Have oysters and lobsters to cure melancholy:
Fish-dinners will make a lass spring like a flea,
Dame Venus, love's lady,
Was born of the sea;
With her and with Bacchus we'll tickle the sense,
For we shall be past it a hundred years hence.

Your most beautiful bride who with garlands is crown'd
And kills with each glance as she treads on the ground,
Whose lightness and brightness doth shine in such splendour
That none but the stars
Are thought fit to attend her,
Though now she be pleasant and sweet to the sense,
Will be damnable mouldy a hundred years hence.

Then why should we turmoil in cares and in fears,
Turn all our tranquill'ty to sighs and to tears?

Let's eat, drink, and play till the worms do corrupt us,
    'Tis certain, *Post mortem*
    Nulla voluptas.
For health, wealth and beauty, wit, learning and sense,
Must all come to nothing a hundred years hence.

40 RICHARD LOVELACE

To Althea, from Prison

When Love with unconfinèd wings
  Hovers within my gates,
And my divine Althea brings
  To whisper at the grates;
When I lie tangled in her hair
  And fetter'd to her eye,
The birds that wanton in the air
  Know no such liberty.

When flowing cups run swiftly round
  With no allaying Thames,
Our careless heads with roses bound,
  Our hearts with loyal flames;
When thirsty grief in wine we steep,
  When healths and draughts go free—
Fishes that tipple in the deep
  Know no such liberty.

When, like committed linnets, I
  With shriller throat shall sing
The sweetness, mercy, majesty,
  And glories of my King;
When I shall voice aloud how good
  He is, how great should be,
Enlargèd winds, that curl the flood,
  Know no such liberty.

Stone walls do not a prison make,
  Nor iron bars a cage;
Minds innocent and quiet take
  That for an hermitage;
If I have freedom in my love
  And in my soul am free,
Angels alone, that soar above,
  Enjoy such liberty.

41 ABRAHAM COWLEY

Drinking

The thirsty earth soaks up the rain,
And drinks and gapes for drink again;
The plants suck in the earth, and are
With constant drinking fresh and fair;
The sea itself (which one would think
Should have but little need of drink)
Drinks twice ten thousand rivers up,
So fill'd that they o'erflow the cup.
The busy Sun (and one would guess
By 's drunken fiery face no less)
Drinks up the sea, and when he's done,
The Moon and Stars drink up the Sun:
They drink and dance by their own light,
They drink and revel all the night:
Nothing in Nature's sober found,
But an eternal health goes round.
Fill up the bowl, then, fill it high,
Fill all the glasses there—for why
Should every creature drink but I?
Why, man of morals, tell me why?

42 ALEXANDER BROME

The Resolve

Tell me not of a face that's fair,
  Nor lip and cheek that's red,
Nor of the tresses of her hair,
  Nor curls in order laid,
Nor of a rare seraphic voice
  That like an angel sings;
Though if I were to take my choice
  I would have all these things:
But if that thou wilt have me love,
  And it must be a she,
The only argument can move
  Is that she will love me.

The glories of your ladies be
  But metaphors of things,
And but resemble what we see
  Each common object brings.
Roses out-red their lips and cheeks,
  Lilies their whiteness stain;
What fool is he that shadows seeks
  And may the substance gain?
Then if thou'lt have me love a lass,
  Let it be one that's kind:
Else I'm a servant to the glass
  That's with Canary lined.

43 ANDREW MARVELL

Thoughts in a Garden

How vainly men themselves amaze
To win the palm, the oak, or bays,
And their uncessant labours see
Crown'd from some single herb or tree,
Whose short and narrow-vergèd shade
Does prudently their toils upbraid;
While all the flowers and trees do close
To weave the garlands of repose!

Fair Quiet, have I found thee here,
And Innocence thy sister dear?
Mistaken long, I sought you then
In busy companies of men:
Your sacred plants, if here below,
Only among the plants will grow:
Society is all but rude
To this delicious solitude.

No white nor red was ever seen
So amorous as this lovely green.
Fond lovers, cruel as their flame,
Cut in these trees their mistress' name:
Little, alas! they know or heed
How far these beauties hers exceed!
Fair trees! wheres'e'er your barks I wound,
No name shall but your own be found.

When we have run our passions' heat,
Love hither makes his best retreat:
The gods, that mortal beauty chase,
Still in a tree did end their race;
Apollo hunted Daphne so
Only that she might laurel grow;
And Pan did after Syrinx speed
Not as a nymph, but for a reed.

What wondrous life in this I lead!
Ripe apples drop about my head;
The luscious clusters of the vine
Upon my mouth do crush their wine;
The nectarine and curious peach
Into my hands themselves do reach;
Stumbling on melons, as I pass,
Ensnared with flowers, I fall on grass.

Meanwhile the mind from pleasure less
Withdraws into its happiness;
The mind, that Ocean where each kind
Does straight its own resemblance find:
Yet it creates, transcending these,
Far other worlds, and other seas;
Annihilating all that's made
To a green thought in a green shade.

Here at the fountain's sliding foot,
Or at some fruit-tree's mossy root,
Casting the body's vest aside,
My soul into the boughs does glide;

There, like a bird, it sits and sings,
Then whets and combs its silver wings,
And, till prepared for longer flight,
Waves in its plumes the various light.

Such was that happy Garden-state
While man there walk'd without a mate:
After a place so pure and sweet,
What other help could yet be meet!
But 'twas beyond a mortal's share
To wander solitary there:
Two paradises 'twere in one,
To live in Paradise alone.

How well the skilful gard'ner drew
Of flowers and herbs this dial new!
Where, from above, the milder sun
Does through a fragrant zodiac run:
And, as it works, th' industrious bee
Computes its time as well as we.
How could such sweet and wholesome hours
Be reckon'd, but with herbs and flowers!

Friends Departed

They are all gone into the world of light!
And I alone sit ling'ring here;
Their very memory is fair and bright,
And my sad thoughts doth clear.

It glows and glitters in my cloudy breast,
Like stars upon some gloomy grove,
Or those faint beams in which this hill is drest
After the sun's remove.

I see them walking in an air of glory,
Whose light doth trample on my days:
My days, which are at best but dull and hoary,
Mere glimmering and decays.

O holy Hope! and high Humility,
High as the heavens above!
These are your walks, and you have show'd them me,
To kindle my cold love.

Dear, beauteous Death! the jewel of the Just,
Shining nowhere, but in the dark;
What mysteries do lie beyond thy dust,
Could man outlook that mark!

He that hath found some fledg'd bird's nest may know,
At first sight, if the bird be flown;

But what fair well or grove he sings in now,
 That is to him unknown.

And yet as Angels in some brighter dreams
 Call to the soul, when man doth sleep:
So some strange thoughts transcend our wonted themes,
 And into glory peep.

If a star were confin'd into a tomb,
 Her captive flames must needs burn there;
But when the hand that lock'd her up gives room,
 She'll shine through all the sphere.

O Father of eternal life, and all
 Created glories under Thee!
Resume Thy spirit from this world of thrall
 Into true liberty.

Either disperse these mists, which blot and fill
 My perspective still as they pass:
Or else remove me hence unto that hill,
 Where I shall need no glass.

45 JOHN DRYDEN

A Song for St. Cecilia's Day, 1687

From harmony, from heavenly harmony,
This universal frame began;
When Nature underneath a heap
Of jarring atoms lay,
And could not heave her head,
The tuneful voice was heard from high,
Arise, ye more than dead!
Then cold and hot, and moist and dry,
In order to their stations leap,
And Music's power obey.
From harmony, from heavenly harmony,
This universal frame began:
From harmony to harmony,
Through all the compass of the notes it ran,
The diapason closing full in man.

What passion cannot Music raise and quell?
When Jubal struck the chorded shell,
His listening brethren stood around,
And, wondering, on their faces fell,
To worship that celestial sound.
Less than a God they thought there could not
dwell
Within the hollow of that shell,
That spoke so sweetly and so well.
What passion cannot Music raise and quell?

The trumpet's loud clangor
Excites us to arms,
With shrill notes of anger,
And mortal alarms.
The double double double beat
Of the thundering drum
Cries, Hark! the foes come;
Charge, charge, 't is too late to retreat!

The soft complaining flute
In dying notes discovers
The woes of hopeless lovers,
Whose dirge is whispered by the warbling lute.

Sharp violins proclaim
Their jealous pangs, and desperation,
Fury, frantic indignation,
Depth of pains, and height of passion
For the fair, disdainful dame.

But O, what art can teach,
What human voice can reach,
The sacred organ's praise?
Notes inspiring holy love,
Notes that wing their heavenly ways
To mend the choirs above.

Orpheus could lead the savage race;
And trees uprooted left their place,
Sequacious of the lyre;

But bright Cecilia raised the wonder higher;
When to her organ vocal breath was given,
An angel heard, and straight appeared
Mistaking earth for heaven.

GRAND CHORUS.

As from the power of sacred lays
The spheres began to move,
And sung the great Creator's praise
To all the blessed above;
So, when the last and dreadful hour
This crumbling pageant shall devour,
The trumpet shall be heard on high,
The dead shall live, the living die,
And Music shall untune the sky.

46 CHARLES SACKVILLE, EARL OF DORSET

The Advice

Phyllis, for shame, let us improve
  A thousand several ways,
These few short minutes stolen by love
  From many tedious days.

Whilst you want courage to despise
  The censure of the grave,
For all the tyrants in your eyes,
  Your heart is but a slave.

My love is full of noble pride,
  And never will submit
To let that fop, Discretion, ride
  In triumph over wit.

False friends I have, as well as you,
  That daily counsel me
Vain frivolous trifles to pursue,
  And leave off loving thee.

When I the least belief bestow
  On what such fools advise,
May I be dull enough to grow
  Most miserably wise.

47. EDWARD TAYLOR

Upon a Wasp Chilled With Cold

The Bear that breaks the Northern blast
Did numb, Torpedo-like, a Wasp
Whose stiffend limbs encrampt, lay bathing
In Sol's warm breath and shine as saving,
Which with her hands she chafes and slams
Rubbing her Legs, Shanks, Thighs, and
hands.
Her petty toes, and fingers ends
Nipt with this breath, she out extends
Unto the Sun, in greate desire
To warm her digits at that fire:
Doth hold her Temples in this state
Where pulse doth beate, and head doth ake:
Doth turn and stretch her body small,
Doth comb her velvet capitall
As if her little brain-pan were
A Volume of choice precepts cleare:
As if her sattin jacket hot
Contained Apothecaries shop
Of Natures recepts, that prevails
To remedy all her sad ailes,
As if her velvet helmet high
Did turret rationality.
She fans her wing up to the winde
As if her Pettycoate were lin'de
With reasons fleece, and hoises saile
And humming flies in thankfull gaile

Unto her dun curld palace Hall,
Her warm thanks offering all.

Lord, cleare my misted sight that I
May hence view thy Divinity,
Some sparkles whereof thou up dost hasp
Within this little downy Wasp,
In whose small Corporation wee
A school and a schoolmaster see:
Where we may learn, and easily finde
A nimble Spirit, bravely minde
Her worke in ev'ry limb: and lace
It up neate with a vitall grace,
Acting each part though ne'er so small,
Here of this fustian animall,
Till I enravisht climb into
The Godhead on this ladder doe:
Where all my pipes inspir'de upraise
An Heavenly musick, furr'd with praise.

48 JOHN WILMOT, EARL OF ROCHESTER

The Disabled Debauchee

As some brave admiral, in former war
  Deprived of force, but pressed with courage still,
Two rival fleets appearing from afar,
  Crawls to the top of an adjacent hill;

From whence, with thoughts full of concern, he views
  The wise and daring conduct of the fight,
Whilst each bold action to his mind renews
  His present glory and his past delight;

From his fierce eyes flashes of fire he throws,
  As from black clouds when lightning breaks away;
Transported, thinks himself amidst the foes,
  And absent, yet enjoys the bloody day;

So, when my days of impotence approach,
  And I'm by pox and wine's unlucky chance
Forced from the pleasing billows of debauch
  On the dull shore of lazy temperance,

My pains at least some respite shall afford
  While I behold the battle you maintain
When fleets of glasses sail about the board,
  From whose broadsides volleys of wit shall rain.

Nor let the sight of honorable scars,
  Which my too forward valor did procure,

Frighten new-listed soldiers from the wars:
  Past joys have more than paid what I endure.

Should any youth (worth being drunk) prove nice,
  And from his fair inviter meanly shrink,
'Twill please the ghost of my departed vice
  If, at my counsel, he repent and drink.

Or should some cold-complexioned sot forbid,
  With his dull morals, our bold night-alarms,
I'll fire his blood by telling what I did
  When I was strong and able to bear arms.

I'll tell of whores attacked, their lords at home;
  Bawds' quarters beaten up, and fortress won:
Windows demolished, watches overcome:
  And handsome ills by my contrivance done.

Nor shall our love-fits, Chloris, be forgot,
  When each the well-looked linkboy strove t' enjoy,
And the best kiss was the deciding lot
  Whether the boy used you, or I the boy.

With tales like these I will such thoughts inspire
  As to important mischief shall incline:
I'll make him long some ancient church to fire,
  And fear no lewdness he's called to by wine.

Thus, statesmanlike, I'll saucily impose,
  And safe from action, valiantly advise;
Sheltered in impotence, urge you to blows,
  And being good for nothing else, be wise.

49 WILLIAM WALSH

Against Marriage

To His Mistress

Yes, all the world must sure agree,
He who's secured of having thee,
  Will be entirely blessed;
But t'were in me too great a wrong,
To make one who has been so long
  My queen, my slave at last.

Nor ought those things to be confined,
That were for public good designed:
  Could we, in foolish pride,
Make the sun always with us stay,
'Twould burn our corn and grass away,
  To starve the world beside.

Let not the thoughts of parting fright
Two souls which passion does unite;
  For while our love does last,
Neither will strive to go away;
And why the devil should we stay,
  When once that love is past?

50 MATTHEW PRIOR

For My Own Monument

As doctors give physic by way of prevention,
  Mat, alive and in health, of his tombstone took care;
For delays are unsafe, and his pious intention
  May haply be never fulfill'd by his heir.

Then take Mat's word for it, the sculptor is paid;
  That the figure is fine, pray believe your own eye;
Yet credit but lightly what more may be said,
  For we flatter ourselves, and teach marble to lie.

Yet counting as far as to fifty his years,
  His virtues and vices as other men's were;
High hopes he conceived, and he smother'd great fears,
  In a life parti-colour'd, half pleasure, half care.

Nor to business a drudge, nor to faction a slave,
  He strove to make int'rest and freedom agree;
In public employments industrious and grave,
  And, alone with his friends, Lord! how merry was he!

Now in equipage stately, now humbly on foot,
  Both fortunes he tried, but to neither would trust;
And whirl'd in the round as the wheel turn'd about,
  He found riches had wings, and knew man was but dust.

This verse, little polish'd, tho' mighty sincere,
  Sets neither his titles nor merit to view;

It says that his relics collected lie here,
  And no mortal yet knows too if this may be true.

Fierce robbers there are that infest the highway,
  So Mat may be kill'd, and his bones never found;
False witness at court, and fierce tempests at sea,
  So Mat may yet chance to be hang'd or be drown'd.

If his bones lie in earth, roll in sea, fly in air,
  To Fate we must yield, and the thing is the same;
And if passing thou giv'st him a smile or a tear,
  He cares not—yet, prithee, be kind to his fame.

51 JONATHAN SWIFT

A Description of a City Shower

Careful observers may foretell the hour
(By sure prognostics) when to dread a shower.
While rain depends, the pensive cat gives o'er
Her frolics, and pursues her tail no more.
Returning home at night, you'll find the sink
Strike your offended sense with double stink.
If you be wise, then go not far to dine;
You'll spend in coach-hire more than save in wine.
A coming shower your shooting corns presage,
Old aches throb, your hollow tooth will rage:
Sauntering in coffee-house is Dulman seen;
He damns the climate and complains of spleen.
  Meanwhile the South, rising with dabbled wings,
A sable cloud athwart the welkin flings,
That swilled more liquor than it could contain,
And, like a drunkard, gives it up again.
Brisk Susan whips her linen from the rope,
While the first drizzling shower is borne aslope:
Such is that sprinkling which some careless quean
Flirts on you from her mop, but not so clean:
You fly, invoke the gods; then turning, stop
To rail; she singing, still whirls on her mop.
Nor yet the dust had shunned the unequal strife,
But, aided by the wind, fought still for life,
And wafted with its foe by violent gust,
'Twas doubtful which was rain and which was dust.
Ah! where must needy poet seek for aid,

When dust and rain at once his coat invade?
Sole coat, where dust cemented by the rain
Erects the nap, and leaves a cloudy stain.
Now in contiguous drops the flood comes down,
Threatening with deluge this devoted town.
To shops in crowds the daggled females fly,
Pretend to cheapen goods, but nothing buy.
The Templar spruce, while every spout's abroach,
Stays till 'tis fair, yet seems to call a coach.
The tucked-up sempstress walks with hasty strides,
While streams run down her oiled umbrella's sides.
Here various kinds, by various fortunes led,
Commence acquaintance underneath a shed.
Triumphant Tories and desponding Whigs
Forget their feuds, and join to save their wigs.
Boxed in a chair the beau impatient sits,
While spouts run clattering o'er the roof by fits;
And ever and anon with frightful din
The leather sounds; he trembles from within.
So when Troy chairmen bore the wooden steed,
Pregnant with Greeks impatient to be freed
(Those bully Greeks, who, as the moderns do,
Instead of paying chairmen, run them through),
Laocoön struck the outside with his spear,
And each imprisoned hero quaked for fear.
Now from all parts the swelling kennels flow,
And bear their trophies with them as they go:
Filth of all hues and odours seem to tell
What street they sailed from, by their sight and smell.
They, as each torrent drives with rapid force,
From Smithfield or St. Pulchre's shape their course,

And in huge confluence joined at Snow Hill ridge,
Fall from the conduit prone to Holborn Bridge.
Sweepings from butchers' stalls, dung, guts, and blood,
Drowned puppies, stinking sprats, all drenched in mud,
Dead cats, and turnip-tops, come tumbling down
the flood.

52 JOHN GAY

To a Lady on Her Passion for Old China

What ecstasies her bosom fire!
How her eyes languish with desire!
How blessed, how happy should I be,
Were that fond glance bestowed on me!
New doubts and fears within me war:
What rival's near? A China jar.
China's the passion of her soul;
A cup, a plate, a dish, a bowl
Can kindle wishes in her breast,
Inflame with joy, or break her rest.
Some gems collect; some medals prize,
And view the rust with lovers' eyes;
Some court the stars at midnight hours;
Some dote on Nature's charms in flowers!
But every beauty I can trace
In Laura's mind, in Laura's face;
My stars are in this brighter sphere,
My lily and my rose is here.
Philosophers more grave than wise
Hunt science down in butterflies;
Or fondly poring on a spider,
Stretch human contemplation wider;
Fossils give joy to Galen's soul;
He digs for knowledge like a mole;
In shells so learned, that all agree
No fish that swims knows more than he!
In such pursuits if wisdom lies,

Who, Laura, shall thy taste despise?
  When I some antique jar behold,
Or white, or blue, or specked with gold,
Vessels so pure and so refined
Appear the types of womankind:
Are they not valued for their beauty,
Too fair, too fine for household duty,
With flowers and gold and azure dyed,
Of every house the grace and pride?
How white, how polished is their skin,
And valued most when only seen!
She who before was highest prized,
Is for a crack or flaw despised;
I grant they're frail, yet they're so rare,
The treasure cannot cost too dear!
But man is made of coarser stuff,
And serves convenience well enough;
He's a strong earthern vessel, made
For drudging, labour, toil, and trade;
And when wives lose their other self,
With ease they bear the loss of Delf.
  Husbands more covetous than sage
Condemn this China-buying rage;
They count that woman's prudence little,
Who sets her heart on things so brittle.
But are those wise men's inclinations
Fixed on more strong, more sure foundations?
If all that's frail we must despise,
No human view or scheme is wise.
Are not Ambition's hopes as weak?
They swell like bubbles, shine, and break.

A courtier's promise is so slight,
'Tis made at noon, and broke at night.
What pleasure's sure? The miss you keep
Breaks both your fortune and your sleep.
The man who loves a country life
Breaks all the comforts of his wife;
And if he quit his farm and plough,
His wife in town may break her vow.
Love, Laura, love, while youth is warm,
For each new winter breaks a charm;
And woman's not like China sold,
But cheaper grows in growing old;
Then quickly choose the prudent part,
Or else you break a faithful heart.

53 ALEXANDER POPE

Ode to Solitude

Happy the man, whose wish and care
  A few paternal acres bound,
Content to breathe his native air,
    In his own ground.

Whose herds with milk, whose fields with bread,
  Whose flocks supply him with attire;
Whose trees in summer yield him shade,
    In winter, fire.

Blest who can unconcern'dly find
  Hours, days, and years slide soft away
In health of body, peace of mind,
    Quiet by day,

Sound sleep by night; study and ease
  Together mixt; sweet recreation,
And Innocence, which most does please
    With meditation.

Thus let me live, unseen, unknown;
  Thus unlamented let me die;
Steal from the world, and not a stone
    Tell where I lie.

54 LADY MARY WORTLEY MONTAGU

The Lover: A Ballad

At length, by so much importunity pressed,
Take, C———, at once, the inside of my breast;
This stupid indifference so often you blame
Is not owing to nature, to fear, or to shame;
I am not as cold as a Virgin in lead,
Nor is Sunday's sermon so strong in my head;
I know but too well how time flies along,
That we live but few years and yet fewer are young.

But I hate to be cheated, and never will buy
Long years of repentance for moments of joy.
Oh was there a man (but where shall I find
Good sense and good nature so equally joined?)
Would value his pleasure, contribute to mine,
Not meanly would boast, nor would lewdly design,
Not over severe, yet not stupidly vain,
For I would have the power though not give the pain;

No pedant yet learned, not rakehelly gay
Or laughing because he has nothing to say,
To all my whole sex obliging and free,
Yet never be fond of any but me;
In public preserve the decorum that's just,
And show in his eyes he is true to his trust,
Then rarely approach, and respectfully bow,
Yet not fulsomely pert, nor yet foppishly low.

But when the long hours of public are past
And we meet with champagne and a chicken at last,
May every fond pleasure that hour endear,
Be banished afar both discretion and fear,
Forgetting or scorning the airs of the crowd
He may cease to be formal, and I to be proud,
Till lost in the joy we confess that we live,
And he may be rude, and yet I may forgive.

And that my delight may be solidly fixed,
Let the friend and the lover be handsomely mixed,
In whose tender bosom my soul might confide,
Whose kindness can sooth me, whose counsel could guide.
From such a dear lover as here I describe
No danger should fright me, no millions should bribe;
But till this astonishing creature I know,
As I long have lived chaste, I will keep myself so.

I never will share with the wanton coquette,
Or be caught by a vain affectation of wit.
The toasters and songsters may try all their art
But never shall enter the pass of my heart.
I loathe the lewd rake, the dressed fopling despise;
Before such pursuers the nice virgin flies;
And as Ovid has sweetly in parables told
We harden like trees, and like rivers are cold.

55 HENRY CAREY

Sally in our Alley

Of all the girls that are so smart
  There's none like pretty Sally;
She is the darling of my heart,
  And she lives in our alley.
There is no lady in the land
  Is half so sweet as Sally;
She is the darling of my heart,
  And she lives in our alley.

Her father he makes cabbage-nets,
  And through the streets does cry 'em;
Her mother she sells laces long
  To such as please to buy 'em:
But sure such folks could ne'er beget
  So sweet a girl as Sally!
She is the darling of my heart,
  And she lives in our alley.

When she is by, I leave my work,
  I love her so sincerely;
My master comes like any Turk,
  And bangs me most severely:
But let him bang his bellyful,
  I'll bear it all for Sally;
She is the darling of my heart,
  And she lives in our alley.

Of all the days that's in the week
  I dearly love but one day—
And that's the day that comes betwixt
  A Saturday and Monday;
For then I'm drest all in my best
  To walk abroad with Sally;
She is the darling of my heart,
  And she lives in our alley.

My master carries me to church,
  And often am I blamèd
Because I leave him in the lurch
  As soon as text is namèd;
I leave the church in sermon-time
  And slink away to Sally;
She is the darling of my heart,
  And she lives in our alley.

When Christmas comes about again,
  O, then I shall have money;
I'll hoard it up, and box it all,
  I'll give it to my honey:
I would it were ten thousand pound,
  I'd give it all to Sally;
She is the darling of my heart,
  And she lives in our alley.

My master and the neighbours all,
  Make game of me and Sally,
And, but for her, I'd better be
  A slave and row a galley;

But when my seven long years are out,
  O, then I'll marry Sally;
O, then we'll wed, and then we'll bed—
  But not in our alley!

56 SAMUEL JOHNSON

One-and-Twenty

Long-expected one-and-twenty,
  Ling'ring year, at length is flown:
Pride and pleasure, pomp and plenty,
  Great*******, are now your own.

Loosen'd from the minor's tether,
  Free to mortgage or to sell,
Wild as wind, and light as feather,
  Bid the sons of thrift farewell.

Call the Betsies, Kates, and Jennies,
  All the names that banish care;
Lavish of your grandsire's guineas,
  Show the spirit of an heir.

All that prey on vice and folly
  Joy to see their quarry fly:
There the gamester, light and jolly,
  There the lender, grave and sly.

Wealth, my lad, was made to wander,
  Let it wander as it will;
Call the jockey, call the pander,
  Bid them come and take their fill.

When the bonny blade carouses,
  Pockets full, and spirits high—

What are acres? What are houses?
  Only dirt, or wet or dry.

Should the guardian friend or mother
  Tell the woes of wilful waste,
Scorn their counsel, scorn their pother;—
  You can hang or drown at last!

57 WILLIAM SHENSTONE

Song

O'er desert plains, and rushy meers,
  And wither'd heaths I rove;
Where tree, nor spire, nor cot appears,
  I pass to meet my love.

But, tho' my path were damask'd o'er
  With beauties e'er so fine;
My busy thoughts would fly before,
  To fix alone—on thine.

No fir-crown'd hills cou'd give delight,
  No palace please mine eye;
No pyramid's aërial height,
  Where mouldering monarchs lie.

Unmov'd, should Eastern kings advance;
  Could I the pageant see:
Splendour might catch one scornful glance,
  Not steal one thought from thee.

Elegy Written in a Country Churchyard

The Curfew tolls the knell of parting day,
  The lowing herd wind slowly o'er the lea,
The plowman homeward plods his weary way,
  And leaves the world to darkness and to me.

Now fades the glimmering landscape on the sight,
  And all the air a solemn stillness holds,
Save where the beetle wheels his droning flight,
  And drowsy tinklings lull the distant folds;

Save that from yonder ivy-mantled tow'r
  The moping owl does to the moon complain
Of such as, wand'ring near her secret bow'r,
  Molest her ancient solitary reign.

Beneath those rugged elms, that yew-tree's shade,
  Where heaves the turf in many a mould'ring heap,
Each in his narrow cell for ever laid,
  The rude Forefathers of the hamlet sleep.

The breezy call of incense-breathing Morn,
  The swallow twitt'ring from the straw-built shed,
The cock's shrill clarion, or the echoing horn,
  No more shall rouse them from their lowly bed.

For them no more the blazing hearth shall burn,
  Or busy housewife ply her evening care:

No children run to lisp their sire's return,
  Or climb his knees the envied kiss to share.

Oft did the harvest to their sickle yield,
  Their furrow oft the stubborn glebe has broke:
How jocund did they drive their team afield!
  How bow'd the woods beneath their sturdy stroke!

Let not Ambition mock their useful toil,
  Their homely joys, and destiny obscure;
Nor Grandeur hear with a disdainful smile
  The short and simple annals of the poor.

The boast of heraldry, the pomp of pow'r,
  And all that beauty, all that wealth e'er gave,
Awaits alike th' inevitable hour:
  The paths of glory lead but to the grave.

Nor you, ye Proud, impute to These the fault,
  If Memory o'er their Tomb no Trophies raise,
Where through the long-drawn aisle and fretted vault
  The pealing anthem swells the note of praise.

Can storied urn or animated bust
  Back to its mansion call the fleeting breath?
Can Honour's voice provoke the silent dust,
  Or Flatt'ry soothe the dull cold ear of death?

Perhaps in this neglected spot is laid
  Some heart once pregnant with celestial fire;

Hands, that the rod of empire might have sway'd,
Or waked to ecstasy the living lyre.

But Knowledge to their eyes her ample page
Rich with the spoils of time did ne'er unroll;
Chill Penury repress'd their noble rage,
And froze the genial current of the soul.

Full many a gem of purest ray serene
The dark unfathom'd caves of ocean bear:
Full many a flower is born to blush unseen,
And waste its sweetness on the desert air.

Some village Hampden that with dauntless breast
The little tyrant of his fields withstood,
Some mute inglorious Milton, here may rest,
Some Cromwell guiltless of his country's blood.

Th' applause of list'ning senates to command,
The threats of pain and ruin to despise,
To scatter plenty o'er a smiling land,
And read their history in a nation's eyes,

Their lot forbade: nor circumscribed alone
Their growing virtues, but their crimes confined:
Forbade to wade through slaughter to a throne,
And shut the gates of mercy on mankind,

The struggling pangs of conscious truth to hide,
To quench the blushes of ingenuous shame,
Or heap the shrine of Luxury and Pride
With incense kindled at the Muse's flame.

Far from the madding crowd's ignoble strife
  Their sober wishes never learn'd to stray;
Along the cool sequester'd vale of life
  They kept the noiseless tenor of their way.

Yet ev'n these bones from insult to protect
  Some frail memorial still erected nigh,
With uncouth rhymes and shapeless sculpture deck'd,
  Implores the passing tribute of a sigh.

Their name, their years, spelt by th' unletter'd muse,
  The place of fame and elegy supply:
And many a holy text around she strews,
  That teach the rustic moralist to die.

For who, to dumb Forgetfulness a prey,
  This pleasing anxious being e'er resign'd,
Left the warm precincts of the cheerful day,
  Nor cast one longing ling'ring look behind?

On some fond breast the parting soul relies,
  Some pious drops the closing eye requires;
E'en from the tomb the voice of Nature cries,
  E'en in our Ashes live their wonted Fires.

For thee, who, mindful of th' unhonour'd dead,
  Dost in these lines their artless tale relate;
If chance, by lonely contemplation led,
  Some kindred spirit shall inquire thy fate,

Haply some hoary-headed Swain may say,
  'Oft have we seen him at the peep of dawn

Brushing with hasty steps the dews away
To meet the sun upon the upland lawn.

'There at the foot of yonder nodding beech
That wreathes its old fantastic roots so high,
His listless length at noontide would he stretch,
And pore upon the brook that babbles by.

'Hard by yon wood, now smiling as in scorn,
Mutt'ring his wayward fancies he would rove,
Now drooping, woeful wan, like one forlorn,
Or crazed with care, or cross'd in hopeless love.

'One morn I miss'd him on the custom'd hill,
Along the heath and near his fav'rite tree;
Another came, nor yet beside the rill,
Nor up the lawn, nor at the wood was he;

'The next with dirges due in sad array
Slow through the church-way path we saw him borne.
Approach and read (for thou canst read) the lay
Graved on the stone beneath yon aged thorn.'

THE EPITAPH

Here rests his head upon the lap of Earth
A Youth to Fortune and to Fame unknown.
Fair Science frown'd not on his humble birth,
And Melancholy mark'd him for her own.

Large was his bounty, and his soul sincere,
Heav'n did a recompense as largely send:
He gave to Mis'ry all he had, a tear,
He gain'd from Heav'n ('twas all he wish'd)
a friend.

No farther seek his merits to disclose,
Or draw his frailties from their dread abode,
(There they alike in trembling hope repose,)
The bosom of his Father and his God.

59 WILLIAM COLLINS

Ode to Evening

If aught of oaten stop, or pastoral song,
May hope, chaste Eve, to soothe thy modest ear,
    Like thy own solemn springs,
    Thy springs and dying gales;

O nymph reserved, while now the bright-hair'd sun
Sits in yon western tent, whose cloudy skirts,
    With brede ethereal wove,
    O'erhang his wavy bed:

Now air is hush'd save where the weak-eyed bat
With short shrill shriek flits by on leathern wing,
    Or where the beetle winds
    His small but sullen horn,

As oft he rises, 'midst the twilight path
Against the pilgrim borne in heedless hum:
    Now teach me, maid composed,
    To breathe some soften'd strain,

Whose numbers, stealing through thy darkening vale,
May not unseemly with its stillness suit,
    As, musing slow, I hail
    Thy genial loved return!

For when thy folding-star arising shows
His paly circlet, at his warning lamp

The fragrant hours, and elves
Who slept in buds the day,

And many a nymph who wreathes her brows with sedge,
And sheds the freshening dew, and, lovelier still,
The pensive pleasures sweet,
Prepare thy shadowy car:

Then lead, calm votaress, where some sheety lake
Cheers the lone heath, or some time-hallow'd pile,
Or upland fallows grey
Reflect its last cool gleam.

Or if chill blustering winds, or driving rain,
Prevent my willing feet, be mine the hut
That from the mountain's side
Views wilds and swelling floods,

And hamlets brown, and dim-discover'd spires,
And hears their simple bell, and marks o'er all
Thy dewy fingers draw
The gradual dusky veil.

While Spring shall pour his show'rs, as oft he wont,
And bathe thy breathing tresses, meekest Eve!
While Summer loves to sport
Beneath thy lingering light;

While sallow Autumn fills thy lap with leaves,
Or Winter, yelling through the troublous air,

Affrights thy shrinking train,
And rudely rends thy robes:

So long, regardful of thy quiet rule,
Shall Fancy, Friendship, Science, rose-lipp'd Health
Thy gentlest influence own,
And hymn thy favourite name!

60 CHRISTOPHER SMART

Adoration

For ADORATION seasons change,
And order, truth and beauty range,
  Adjust, attract, and fill:
The grass the polyanthus cheques;
And polish'd porphyry reflects,
  By the descending rill.

Rich almonds colour to the prime
For ADORATION; tendrils climb,
  And fruit-trees pledge their gems;
And Ivis, with her gorgeous vest,
Builds for her eggs her cunning nest,
  And bell-flowers bow their stems.

With vinous syrup cedars spout;
From rocks pure honey gushing out,
  For ADORATION springs:
All scenes of painting croud the map
Of nature; to the mermaid's pap
  The scaled infant clings.

The spotted ounce and playsome cubs
Run rustling 'mongst the flow'ring shrubs,
  And lizards feed the moss;
For ADORATION beasts embark,
While waves upholding halcyon's ark
  No longer roar and toss.

While Israel sits beneath his fig,
With coral root and amber sprig
  The wean'd advent'rer sports;
Where to the palm the jasmin cleaves,
For ADORATION 'mongst the leaves
  The gale his peace reports.

Increasing days their reign exalt,
Nor in the pink and mottled vault
  The opposing spirits tilt;
And, by the coasting reader spied,
The silverlings and crusions glide
  For ADORATION gilt.

For ADORATION rip'ning canes,
And cocoa's purest milk detains
  The western pilgrim's staff;
Where rain in clasping boughs inclos'd,
And vines with oranges dispos'd,
  Embow'r the social laugh.

Now labour his reward receives,
For ADORATION counts his sheaves,
  To peace, her bounteous prince;
The nectarine his strong tint imbibes,
And apples of ten thousand tribes,
  And quick peculiar quince.

The wealthy crops of whit'ning rice,
'Mongst thyine woods and groves of spice,
  For ADORATION grow;

And, marshall'd in the fenced land,
The peaches and pomegranates stand,
Where wild carnations blow.

The laurels with the winter strive;
The crocus burnishes alive
Upon the snow-clad earth:
For ADORATION myrtles stay
To keep the garden from dismay,
And bless the sight from dearth.

The pheasant shows his pompous neck;
And ermine, jealous of a speck,
With fear eludes offence:
The sable with his glossy pride,
For ADORATION is descried,
Where frosts the waves condense.

The chearful holly, pensive yew,
And holy thorn, their trim renew;
The squirrel hoards his nuts:
All creatures batten o'er their stores,
And careful nature all her doors
For ADORATION shuts.

61 WILLIAM BLAKE

London

I wander through each chartered street,
Near where the chartered Thames does flow,
And mark in every face I meet
Marks of weakness, marks of woe.

In every cry of every Man,
In every Infant's cry of fear,
In every voice, in every ban,
The mind-forged manacles I hear.

How the chimney-sweeper's cry
Every blackening church appalls;
And the hapless soldier's sigh
Runs in blood down palace walls.

But most through midnight streets I hear
How the youthful harlot's curse
Blasts the new-born infant's tear,
And blights with plagues the marriage hearse.

My Bonnie Mary

Go fetch to me a pint o' wine,
  An' fill it in a silver tassie,
That I may drink, before I go,
  A service to my bonnie lassie.
The boat rocks at the pier o' Leith,
  Fu' loud the wind blaws frae the ferry,
The ship rides by the Berwick-law,
  And I maun leave my bonnie Mary.

The trumpets sound, the banners fly,
  The glittering spears are rankèd ready;
The shouts o' war are heard afar,
  The battle closes thick and bloody;
But it's no the roar o' sea or shore
  Wad mak me langer wish to tarry;
Nor shout o' war that's heard afar—
  It's leaving thee, my bonnie Mary!

63 SAMUEL ROGERS

A Wish

Mine be a cot beside the hill;
A beehive's hum shall soothe my ear;
A willowy brook that turns a mill,
With many a fall shall linger near.

The swallow, oft, beneath my thatch
Shall twitter from her clay-built nest;
Oft shall the pilgrim lift the latch,
And share my meal, a welcome guest.

Around my ivied porch shall spring
Each fragrant flower that drinks the dew,
And Lucy, at her wheel, shall sing
In russet gown and apron blue.

The village-church among the trees,
Where first our marriage-vows were given,
With merry peals shall swell the breeze
And point with taper spire to heaven.

64 WILLIAM WORDSWORTH

Lucy (v)

A slumber did my spirit seal;
   I had no human fears:
She seem'd a thing that could not feel
   The touch of earthly years.

No motion has she now, no force;
   She neither hears nor sees;
Roll'd round in earth's diurnal course,
   With rocks, and stones, and trees.

65 SAMUEL TAYLOR COLERIDGE

Kubla Khan

In Xanadu did Kubla Khan
  A stately pleasure-dome decree:
Where Alph, the sacred river, ran
Through caverns measureless to man
  Down to a sunless sea.
So twice five miles of fertile ground
With walls and towers were girdled round
And there were gardens bright with sinuous rills
Where blossom'd many an incense-bearing tree;
And here were forests ancient as the hills,
Enfolding sunny spots of greenery.

But O, that deep romantic chasm which slanted
Down the green hill athwart a cedarn cover!
A savage place! as holy and enchanted
As e'er beneath a waning moon was haunted
By woman wailing for her demon-lover!
And from this chasm, with ceaseless turmoil seething,
As if this earth in fast thick pants were breathing,
A mighty fountain momently was forced;
Amid whose swift half-intermitted burst
Huge fragments vaulted like rebounding hail,
Or chaffy grain beneath the thresher's flail:
And 'mid these dancing rocks at once and ever
It flung up momently the sacred river.
Five miles meandering with a mazy motion

Through wood and dale the sacred river ran,
Then reach'd the caverns measureless to man,
And sank in tumult to a lifeless ocean:
And 'mid this tumult Kubla heard from far
Ancestral voices prophesying war!

The shadow of the dome of pleasure
Floated midway on the waves;
Where was heard the mingled measure
From the fountain and the caves.
It was a miracle of rare device,
A sunny pleasure-dome with caves of ice!

A damsel with a dulcimer
In a vision once I saw:
It was an Abyssinian maid,
And on her dulcimer she play'd,
Singing of Mount Abora.
Could I revive within me,
Her symphony and song,
To such a deep delight 'twould win me,
That with music loud and long,
I would build that dome in air,
That sunny dome! those caves of ice!
And all who heard should see them there,
And all should cry, Beware! Beware!
His flashing eyes, his floating hair!

Weave a circle round him thrice,
And close your eyes with holy dread,
For he on honey-dew hath fed,
And drunk the milk of Paradise.

66 WALTER SAVAGE LANDOR

Rose Aylmer

Ah, what avails the sceptred race!
  Ah, what the form divine!
What every virtue, every grace!
  Rose Aylmer, all were thine.

Rose Aylmer, whom these wakeful eyes
  May weep, but never see,
A night of memories and sighs
  I consecrate to thee.

67 LEIGH HUNT

The Fish, the Man, and the Spirit

TO A FISH

You strange, astonished-looking, angle-faced,
Dreary-mouthed, gaping wretches of the sea,
Gulping salt-water everlastingly,
Cold-blooded, though with red your blood be graced,
And mute, though dwellers in the roaring waste;
And you, all shapes beside, that fishy be—
Some round, some flat, some long, all devilry,
Legless, unloving, infamously chaste—

O scaly, slippery, wet, swift, staring wights,
What is't ye do? what life lead? eh, dull goggles?
How do ye vary your vile days and nights?
How pass your Sundays? Are ye still but joggles
In ceaseless wash? Still nought but gapes, and bites,
And drinks, and stares, diversified with boggles?

A FISH ANSWERS

Amazing monster! that, for aught I know,
With the first sight of thee didst make our race
Forever stare! Oh flat and shocking face,
Grimly divided from the breast below!
Thou that on dry land horribly dost go
With a split body and most ridiculous pace,
Prong after prong, disgracer of all grace,
Long-useless-finned, haired, upright, unwet, slow!

O breather of unbreathable, sword-sharp air,
How canst exist? How bear thyself, thou dry
And dreary sloth? What particle canst share
Of the only blessed life, the watery?
I sometimes see of ye an actual *pair*
Go by! linked fin by fin! most odiously.

THE FISH TURNS INTO A MAN, AND THEN INTO A SPIRIT, AND AGAIN SPEAKS

Indulge thy smiling scorn, if smiling still,
O man! and loathe, but with a sort of love;
For difference must its use by difference prove,
And, in sweet clang, the spheres with music fill.
One of the spirits am I, that at his will
Live in whate'er has life—fish, eagle, dove—
No hate, no pride, beneath nought, nor above,
A visitor of the rounds of God's sweet skill.

Man's life is warm, glad, sad, 'twixt loves and graves,
Boundless in hope, honored with pangs austere,
Heaven-gazing; and his angel-wings he craves:
The fish is swift, small-needing, vague yet clear,
A cold, sweet, silver life, wrapped in round waves,
Quickened with touches of transporting fear.

68 THOMAS LOVE PEACOCK

The War Song of Dinas Vawr

The mountain sheep are sweeter,
But the valley sheep are fatter;
We therefore deemed it meeter
To carry off the latter.
We made an expedition;
We met a host, and quelled it;
We forced a strong position,
And killed the men who held it.

On Dyfed's richest valley,
Where herds of kine were browsing,
We made a mighty sally,
To furnish our carousing.
Fierce warriors rushed to meet us;
We met them, and o'erthrew them:
They struggled hard to beat us;
But we conquered them, and slew them.

As we drove our prize at leisure,
The king marched forth to catch us:
His rage surpassed all measure,
But his people could not match us.
He fled to his hall pillars;
And, ere our force we led off,
Some sacked his house and cellars,
While others cut his head off.

We there, in strife bewild'ring,
Spilt blood enough to swim in:
We orphaned many children,
And widowed many women.
The eagles and the ravens
We glutted with our foemen;
The heroes and the cravens,
The spearmen and the bowmen.

We brought away from battle,
And much their land bemoaned them,
Two thousand head of cattle,
And the head of him who owned them:
Ednyfed, king of Dyfed,
His head was borne before us;
His wine and beasts supplied our feasts,
And his overthrow, our chorus.

69 GEORGE GORDON, LORD BYRON

The Sea

There is a pleasure in the pathless woods,
There is a rapture on the lonely shore,
There is society where none intrudes
By the deep sea, and music in its roar:
I love not man the less, but nature more,
From these our interviews, in which I steal
From all I may be, or have been before,
To mingle with the universe, and feel
What I can ne'er express, yet cannot all conceal.

Roll on, thou deep and dark blue Ocean,—roll!
Ten thousand fleets sweep over thee in vain;
Man marks the earth with ruin,—his control
Stops with the shore;—upon the watery plain
The wrecks are all thy deed, nor doth remain
A shadow of man's ravage, save his own,
When, for a moment, like a drop of rain,
He sinks into thy depths with bubbling groan,
Without a grave, unknelled, uncoffined, and unknown.

His steps are not upon thy paths,—thy fields
Are not a spoil for him,—thou dost arise
And shake him from thee; the vile strength he wields
For earth's destruction thou dost all despise,
Spurning him from thy bosom to the skies,
And send'st him, shivering in thy playful spray

And howling, to his gods, where haply lies
His petty hope in some near port or bay,
And dashest him again to earth:—there let him lay.

The armaments which thunderstrike the walls
Of rock-built cities, bidding nations quake
And monarchs tremble in their capitals,
The oak leviathans, whose huge ribs make
Their clay creator the vain title take
Of lord of thee and arbiter of war,—
These are thy toys, and, as the snowy flake,
They melt into thy yeast of waves, which mar
Alike the Armada's pride or spoils of Trafalgar.

Thy shores are empires, changed in all save thee;
Assyria, Greece, Rome, Carthage, what are they?
Thy waters wasted them while they were free,
And many a tyrant since; their shores obey
The stranger, slave, or savage; their decay
Has dried up realms to deserts: not so thou;
Unchangeable save to thy wild waves' play,
Time writes no wrinkles on thine azure brow;
Such as creation's dawn beheld, thou rollest now.

Thou glorious mirror, where the Almighty's form
Glasses itself in tempests; in all time,
Calm or convulsed,—in breeze, or gale, or storm,
Icing the pole, or in the torrid clime
Dark-heaving; boundless, endless, and sublime,
The image of Eternity,—the throne
Of the Invisible! even from out thy slime

The monsters of the deep are made; each zone
Obeys thee; thou goest forth, dread, fathomless, alone.

And I have loved thee, Ocean! and my joy
Of youthful sports was on thy breast to be
Borne, like thy bubbles, onward; from a boy
I wantoned with thy breakers,—they to me
Were a delight; and if the freshening sea
Made them a terror, 't was a pleasing fear;
For I was as it were a child of thee,
And trusted to thy billows far and near,
And laid my hand upon thy mane,—as I do here.

Ode to the West Wind

I

O Wild West Wind, thou breath of Autumn's being
  Thou from whose unseen presence the leaves dead
Are driven like ghosts from an enchanter fleeing,

  Yellow, and black, and pale, and hectic red,
Pestilence-stricken multitudes! O thou
  Who chariotest to their dark wintry bed

The wingèd seeds, where they lie cold and low,
  Each like a corpse within its grave, until
Thine azure sister of the Spring shall blow

  Her clarion o'er the dreaming earth, and fill
(Driving sweet buds like flocks to feed in air)
  With living hues and odours plain and hill;

Wild Spirit, which art moving everywhere;
Destroyer and preserver; hear, O hear!

II

Thou on whose stream, 'mid the steep sky's commotion,
  Loose clouds like earth's decaying leaves are shed,
Shook from the tangled boughs of heaven and ocean,

  Angels of rain and lightning! there are spread
On the blue surface of thine airy surge,
  Like the bright hair uplifted from the head

Of some fierce Maenad, even from the dim verge
  Of the horizon to the zenith's height,
The locks of the approaching storm. Thou dirge

Of the dying year, to which this closing night
Will be the dome of a vast sepulchre,
Vaulted with all thy congregated might

Of vapours, from whose solid atmosphere
Black rain, and fire, and hail, will burst: O hear!

III

Thou who didst waken from his summer dreams
The blue Mediterranean, where he lay,
Lull'd by the coil of his crystalline streams,

Beside a pumice isle in Baiae's bay,
And saw in sleep old palaces and towers
Quivering within the wave's intenser day,

All overgrown with azure moss, and flowers
So sweet, the sense faints picturing them! Thou
For whose path the Atlantic's level powers

Cleave themselves into chasms, while far below
The sea-blooms and the oozy woods which wear
The sapless foliage of the ocean, know

Thy voice, and suddenly grow gray with fear,
And tremble and despoil themselves: O hear!

IV

If I were a dead leaf thou mightest bear;
If I were a swift cloud to fly with thee;
A wave to pant beneath thy power, and share

The impulse of thy strength, only less free
Than thou, O uncontrollable! if even
I were as in my boyhood, and could be

The comrade of thy wanderings over heaven,
As then, when to outstrip thy skiey speed
Scarce seem'd a vision—I would ne'er have striven

As thus with thee in prayer in my sore need.
O! lift me as a wave, a leaf, a cloud!
I fall upon the thorns of life! I bleed!

A heavy weight of hours has chain'd and bow'd
One too like thee—tameless, and swift, and proud.

V

Make me thy lyre, even as the forest is:
What if my leaves are falling like its own?
The tumult of thy mighty harmonies

Will take from both a deep autumnal tone,
Sweet though in sadness. Be thou, Spirit fierce,
My spirit! Be thou me, impetuous one!

Drive my dead thoughts over the universe,
Like wither'd leaves, to quicken a new birth;
And, by the incantation of this verse,

Scatter, as from an unextinguish'd hearth
Ashes and sparks, my words among mankind!
Be through my lips to unawaken'd earth

The trumpet of a prophecy! O Wind,
If Winter comes, can Spring be far behind?

71 JOHN CLARE

Written in Northampton County Asylum

I am! yet what I am who cares, or knows?
  My friends forsake me like a memory lost.
I am the self-consumer of my woes;
  They rise and vanish, an oblivious host,
Shadows of life, whose very soul is lost.
And yet I am—I live—though I am toss'd

Into the nothingness of scorn and noise,
  Into the living sea of waking dream,
Where there is neither sense of life, nor joys,
  But the huge shipwreck of my own esteem
And all that's dear. Even those I loved the best
Are strange—nay, they are stranger than the rest.

I long for scenes where man has never trod—
  For scenes where woman never smiled or wept—
There to abide with my Creator, God,
  And sleep as I in childhood sweetly slept,
Full of high thoughts, unborn. So let me lie,—
The grass below; above, the vaulted sky.

Thanatopsis

To him who in the love of Nature holds
Communion with her visible forms, she speaks
A various language; for his gayer hours
She has a voice of gladness, and a smile
And eloquence of beauty, and she glides
Into his darker musings, with a mild
And healing sympathy, that steals away
Their sharpness, ere he is aware. When thoughts
Of the last bitter hour come like a blight
Over thy spirit, and sad images
Of the stern agony, and shroud, and pall,
And breathless darkness, and the narrow house,
Make thee to shudder and grow sick at heart;—
Go forth, under the open sky, and list
To Nature's teachings, while from all around—
Earth and her waters, and the depths of air—
Comes a still voice—Yet a few days, and thee
The all-beholding sun shall see no more
In all his course; nor yet in the cold ground,
Where thy pale form was laid with many tears,
Nor in the embrace of ocean, shall exist
Thy image. Earth, that nourish'd thee, shall claim
Thy growth, to be resolved to earth again,
And, lost each human trace, surrendering up
Thine individual being, shalt thou go
To mix for ever with the elements,
To be a brother to the insensible rock,

And to the sluggish clod, which the rude swain
Turns with his share, and treads upon. The oak
Shall send his roots abroad, and pierce thy mould.

Yet not to thine eternal resting-place
Shalt thou retire alone, nor couldst thou wish
Couch more magnificent. Thou shalt lie down
With patriarchs of the infant world—with kings,
The powerful of the earth—the wise, the good,
Fair forms, and hoary seers of ages past,
All in one mighty sepulchre. The hills
Rock-ribb'd and ancient as the sun,—the vales
Stretching in pensive quietness between;
The venerable woods; rivers that move
In majesty, and the complaining brooks
That make the meadows green; and, pour'd round all,
Old Ocean's grey and melancholy waste,—
Are but the solemn decorations all
Of the great tomb of man. The golden sun,
The planets, all the infinite host of heaven,
Are shining on the sad abodes of death,
Through the still lapse of ages. All that tread
The globe are but a handful to the tribes
That slumber in its bosom.—Take the wings
Of morning, pierce the Barcan wilderness,
Or lose thyself in the continuous woods
Where rolls the Oregon and hears no sound
Save his own dashings—yet the dead are there:
And millions in those solitudes, since first
The flight of years began, have laid them down
In their last sleep—the dead reign there alone.

So shalt thou rest: and what if thou withdraw
In silence from the living, and no friend
Take note of thy departure? All that breathe
Will share thy destiny. The gay will laugh
When thou art gone, the solemn brood of care
Plod on, and each one as before will chase
His favourite phantom; yet all these shall leave
Their mirth and their employments, and shall come
And make their bed with thee. As the long train
Of ages glide away, the sons of men,
The youth in life's green spring, and he who goes
In the full strength of years, matron and maid,
The speechless babe, and the grey-headed man—
Shall one by one be gathered to thy side
By those who in their turn shall follow them.

So live, that when thy summons comes to join
The innumerable caravan which moves
To that mysterious realm where each shall take
His chamber in the silent halls of death,
Thou go not, like the quarry-slave at night,
Scourged to his dungeon; but, sustain'd and soothed
By an unfaltering trust, approach thy grave,
Like one who wraps the drapery of his couch
About him, and lies down to pleasant dreams.

73 JOHN KEATS

The Eve of St. Agnes

St. Agnes' Eve—Ah, bitter chill it was!
The owl, for all his feathers, was a-cold;
The hare limped trembling through the frozen grass,
And silent was the flock in woolly fold:
Numb were the Beadsman's fingers while he told
His rosary, and while his frosted breath,
Like pious incense from a censer old,
Seemed taking flight for heaven, without a death,
Past the sweet Virgin's picture, while his prayer he saith.

2

His prayer he saith, this patient, holy man;
Then takes his lamp, and riseth from his knees,
And back returneth, meager, barefoot, wan,
Along the chapel aisle by slow degrees:
The sculptured dead, on each side, seem to freeze,
Imprisoned in black, purgatorial rails:
Knights, ladies, praying in dumb orat'ries,
He passeth by, and his weak spirit fails
To think how they may ache in icy hoods and mails.

3

Northward he turneth through a little door,
And scarce three steps, ere Music's golden tongue
Flattered to tears this aged man and poor;

But no—already had his death-bell rung:
The joys of all his life were said and sung;
His was harsh penance on St. Agnes' Eve:
Another way he went, and soon among
Rough ashes sat he for his soul's reprieve,
And all night kept awake, for sinners' sake to grieve.

4

That ancient Beadsman heard the prelude soft;
And so it chanced, for many a door was wide,
From hurry to and fro. Soon, up aloft,
The silver, snarling trumpets 'gan to chide:
The level chambers, ready with their pride,
Were glowing to receive a thousand guests:
The carved angels, ever eager-eyed,
Stared, where upon their heads the cornice rests,
With hair blown back and wings put crosswise on
their breasts.

5

At length burst in the argent revelry,
With plume, tiara, and all rich array,
Numerous as shadows haunting faerily
The brain new-stuffed, in youth, with triumphs gay
Of old romance. These let us wish away,
And turn, sole-thoughted, to one Lady there,
Whose heart had brooded, all that wintry day,
On love, and winged St. Agnes' saintly care,
As she had heard old dames full many times declare.

6

They told her how, upon St. Agnes' Eve,
Young virgins might have visions of delight,
And soft adorings from their loves receive
Upon the honeyed middle of the night,
If ceremonies due they did aright;
As, supperless to bed they must retire,
And couch supine their beauties, lily white;
Nor look behind, nor sideways, but require
Of Heaven with upward eyes for all that they desire.

7

Full of this whim was thoughtful Madeline:
The music, yearning like a God in pain,
She scarcely heard: her maiden eyes divine,
Fixed on the floor, saw many a sweeping train
Pass by—she heeded not at all: in vain
Came many a tiptoe, amorous cavalier,
And back retired; not cooled by high disdain,
But she saw not: her heart was otherwhere;
She sighed for Agnes' dreams, the sweetest of the year.

8

She danced along with vague, regardless eyes,
Anxious her lips, her breathing quick and short:
The hallowed hour was near at hand: she sighs
Amid the timbrels, and the thronged resort
Of whisperers in anger or in sport;
'Mid looks of love, defiance, hate, and scorn,

Hoodwinked with faery fancy; all amort,
Save to St. Agnes and her lambs unshorn,
And all the bliss to be before to-morrow morn.

9

So, purposing each moment to retire,
She lingered still. Meantime, across the moors,
Had come young Porphyro, with heart on fire
For Madeline. Beside the portal doors,
Buttressed from moonlight, stands he, and implores
All saints to give him sight of Madeline,
But for one moment in the tedious hours,
That he might gaze and worship all unseen;
Perchance speak, kneel, touch, kiss—in sooth such
things have been.

10

He ventures in: let no buzzed whisper tell:
All eyes be muffled, or a hundred swords
Will storm his heart, Love's fev'rous citadel:
For him, those chambers held barbarian hordes,
Hyena foemen, and hot-blooded lords,
Whose very dogs would execrations howl
Against his lineage: not one breast affords
Him any mercy, in that mansion foul,
Save one old beldame, weak in body and in soul.

11

Ah, happy chance! the aged creature came,
Shuffling along with ivory-headed wand,

To where he stood, hid from the torch's flame,
Behind a broad hall-pillar, far beyond
The sound of merriment and chorus bland:
He startled her; but soon she knew his face,
And grasped his fingers in her palsied hand,
Saying, "Mercy, Porphyro! hie thee from this place;
They are all here to-night, the whole bloodthirsty race!

12

"Get hence! get hence! there's dwarfish Hildebrand:
He had a fever late, and in the fit
He cursed thee and thine, both house and land:
Then there's that old Lord Maurice, not a whit
More tame for his gray hairs—Alas me! flit!
Flit like a ghost away."—"Ah, Gossip dear,
We're safe enough; here in this arm-chair sit,
And tell me how—" "Good saints! not here, not here!
Follow me, child, or else these stones will be thy bier."

13

He followed through a lowly arched way,
Brushing the cobwebs with his lofty plume;
And as she muttered "Well-a—well-a-day!"
He found him in a little moonlight room,
Pale, latticed, chill, and silent as a tomb.
"Now tell me where is Madeline," said he,
"O tell me, Angela, by the holy loom
Which none but secret sisterhood may see,
When they St. Agnes' wool are weaving piously."

14

"St. Agnes! Ah! it is St. Agnes' Eve—
Yet men will murder upon holy days.
Thou must hold water in a witch's sieve,
And be liege-lord of all the Elves and Fays
To venture so: it fills me with amaze
To see thee, Porphyro!—St. Agnes' Eve!
God's help! my lady fair the conjurer plays
This very night: good angels her deceive!
But let me laugh awhile,—I've mickle time to grieve."

15

Feebly she laugheth in the languid moon,
While Porphyro upon her face doth look,
Like puzzled urchin on an aged crone
Who keepeth closed a wondrous riddle-book,
As spectacled she sits in chimney nook.
But soon his eyes grew brilliant, when she told
His lady's purpose; and he scarce could brook
Tears, at the thought of those enchantments cold,
And Madeline asleep in lap of legends old.

16

Sudden a thought came like a full-blown rose,
Flushing his brow, and in his pained heart
Made purple riot: then doth he propose
A stratagem, that makes the beldame start:
"A cruel man and impious thou art:
Sweet lady, let her pray, and sleep, and dream

Alone with her good angels, far apart
From wicked men like thee. Go, go! I deem
Thou canst not surely be the same that thou didst seem."

17

"I will not harm her, by all saints I swear,"
Quoth Porphyro: "O may I ne'er find grace
When my weak voice shall whisper its last prayer,
If one of her soft ringlets I displace,
Or look with ruffian passion in her face:
Good Angela, believe me by these tears;
Or I will, even in a moment's space,
Awake, with horrid shout, my foemen's ears,
And beard them, though they be more fanged than wolves
and bears."

18

"Ah! why wilt thou affright a feeble soul?
A poor, weak, palsy-stricken, churchyard thing,
Whose passing-bell may ere the midnight toll;
Whose prayers for thee, each morn and evening,
Were never missed." Thus plaining, doth she bring
A gentler speech from burning Porphyro;
So woeful, and of such deep sorrowing,
That Angela gives promise she will do
Whatever he shall wish, betide her weal or woe.

19

Which was, to lead him, in close secrecy,
Even to Madeline's chamber, and there hide

Him in a closet, of such privacy
That he might see her beauty unespied,
And win perhaps that night a peerless bride,
While legioned fairies paced the coverlet,
And pale enchantment held her sleepy-eyed.
Never on such a night have lovers met,
Since Merlin paid his Demon all the monstrous debt.

20

"It shall be as thou wishest," said the Dame:
"All cates and dainties shall be stored there
Quickly on this feast-night: by the tambour frame
Her own lute thou wilt see: no time to spare,
For I am slow and feeble, and scarce dare
On such a catering trust my dizzy head.
Wait here, my child, with patience; kneel in prayer
The while. Ah! thou must needs the lady wed,
Or may I never leave my grave among the dead."

21

So saying she hobbled off with busy fear.
The lover's endless minutes slowly passed;
The dame returned, and whispered in his ear
To follow her; with aged eyes aghast
From fright of dim espial. Safe at last
Through many a dusky gallery, they gain
The maiden's chamber, silken, hushed and chaste;
Where Porphyro took covert, pleased amain.
His poor guide hurried back with agues in her brain.

22

Her faltering hand upon the balustrade,
Old Angela was feeling for the stair,
When Madeline, St. Agnes' charmed maid,
Rose, like a missioned spirit, unaware:
With silver taper's light, and pious care,
She turned, and down the aged gossip led
To a safe level matting. Now prepare,
Young Porphyro, for gazing on that bed;
She comes, she comes again, like ring-dove frayed and fled.

23

Out went the taper as she hurried in;
Its little smoke, in pallid moonshine, died:
She closed the door, she panted, all akin
To spirits of the air, and visions wide:
No uttered syllable, or, woe betide!
But to her heart, her heart was voluble,
Paining with eloquence her balmy side;
As though a tongueless nightingale should swell
Her throat in vain, and die, heart-stifled, in her dell.

24

A casement high and triple-arched there was,
All garlanded with carven imageries,
Of fruits, and flowers, and bunches of knot-grass,
And diamonded with panes of quaint device,
Innumerable of stains and splendid dyes,
As are the tiger-moth's deep-damasked wings;

And in the midst, 'mong thousand heraldries,
And twilight saints, and dim emblazonings,
A shielded scutcheon blushed with blood of queens
and kings.

25

Full on this casement shone the wintry moon,
And threw warm gules on Madeline's fair breast,
As down she knelt for Heaven's grace and boon;
Rose-bloom fell on her hands, together prest,
And on her silver cross soft amethyst,
And on her hair a glory, like a saint:
She seemed a splendid angel, newly drest,
Save wings, for heaven:—Porphyro grew faint:
She knelt, so pure a thing, so free from mortal taint.

26

Anon his heart revives: her vespers done,
Of all its wreathed pearls her hair she frees;
Unclasps her warmed jewels one by one;
Loosens her fragrant bodice; by degrees
Her rich attire creeps rustling to her knees:
Half-hidden, like a mermaid in sea-weed,
Pensive awhile she dreams awake, and sees,
In fancy, fair St. Agnes in her bed,
But dares not look behind, or all the charm is fled.

27

Soon, trembling in her soft and chilly nest,
In sort of wakeful swoon, perplexed she lay,

Until the poppied warmth of sleep oppressed
Her soothed limbs, and soul fatigued away;
Flown, like a thought, until the morrow-day;
Blissfully havened both from joy and pain;
Clasped like a missal where swart Paynims pray;
Blinded alike from sunshine and from rain,
As though a rose should shut, and be a bud again.

28

Stolen to this paradise, and so entranced,
Porphyro gazed upon her empty dress,
And listened to her breathing, if it chanced
To wake into a slumberous tenderness;
Which when he heard, that minute did he bless,
And breathed himself: then from the closet crept,
Noiseless as fear in a wide wilderness,
And over the hushed carpet, silent, stept,
And 'tween the curtains peeped, where, lo!—how
fast she slept.

29

Then by the bed-side, where the faded moon
Made a dim, silver twilight, soft he set
A table, and, half anguished, threw thereon
A cloth of woven crimson, gold, and jet—
O for some drowsy Morphean amulet!
The boisterous, midnight, festive clarion,
The kettle-drum, and far-heard clarinet,
Affray his ears, though but in dying tone:—
The hall-door shuts again, and all the noise is gone.

30

And still she slept an azure-lidded sleep,
In blanched linen, smooth, and lavendered.
While he from forth the closet brought a heap
Of candied apple, quince, and plum, and gourd;
With jellies soother than the creamy curd,
And lucent syrops, tinct with cinnamon;
Manna and dates, in argosy transferred
From Fez; and spiced dainties, every one,
From silken Samarcand to cedared Lebanon.

31

These delicates he heaped with glowing hand
On golden dishes and in baskets bright
Of wreathed silver: sumptuous they stand
In the retired quiet of the night,
Filling the chilly room with perfume light.—
"And now, my love, my seraph fair, awake!
Thou art my heaven, and I thine eremite:
Open thine eyes, for meek St. Agnes' sake,
Or I shall drowse beside thee, so my soul doth ache."

32

Thus whispering, his warm, unnerved arm
Sank in her pillow. Shaded was her dream
By the dusk curtains:—'twas a midnight charm
Impossible to melt as iced stream:
The lustrous salvers in the moonlight gleam;
Broad golden fringe upon the carpet lies:

It seemed he never, never could redeem
From such a stedfast spell his lady's eyes;
So mused awhile, entoiled in woofed phantasies.

33

Awakening up, he took her hollow lute,—
Tumultuous,—and, in chords that tenderest be,
He played an ancient ditty, long since mute,
In Provence called, "La belle dame sans mercy:"
Close to her ear touching the melody:—
Wherewith disturbed, she uttered a soft moan:
He ceased—she panted quick—and suddenly
Her blue affrayed eyes wide open shone:
Upon his knees he sank, pale as smooth-sculptured stone.

34

Her eyes were open, but she still beheld,
Now wide awake, the vision of her sleep:
There was a painful change, that nigh expelled
The blisses of her dream so pure and deep
At which fair Madeline began to weep,
And moan forth witless words with many a sigh,
While still her gaze on Porphyro would keep;
Who knelt, with joined hands and piteous eye,
Fearing to move or speak, she looked so dreamingly.

35

"Ah, Porphyro!" said she, "but even now
Thy voice was at sweet tremble in mine ear,

Made tuneable with every sweetest vow;
And those sad eyes were spiritual and clear:
How changed thou art! how pallid, chill, and drear!
Give me that voice again, my Porphyro,
Those looks immortal, those complainings dear!
Oh, leave me not in this eternal woe,
For if thou diest, my Love, I know not where to go."

36

Beyond a mortal man impassioned far
At these voluptuous accents, he arose,
Ethereal, flushed, and like a throbbing star
Seen 'mid the sapphire heaven's deep repose;
Into her dream he melted, as the rose
Blendeth its odor with the violet,—
Solution sweet: meantime the frost-wind blows
Like Love's alarum, pattering the sharp sleet
Against the window-panes; St. Agnes' moon hath set.

37

'Tis dark: quick pattereth the flaw-blown sleet.
"This is no dream, my bride, my Madeline!"
'Tis dark: the iced gusts still rave and beat:
"No dream, alas! alas! and woe is mine!
Porphyro will leave me here to fade and pine.
Cruel! what traitor could thee hither bring?
I curse not, for my heart is lost in thine,
Though thou forsakest a deceived thing;—
A dove forlorn and lost with sick unpruned wing."

38

"My Madeline! sweet dreamer! lovely bride!
Say, may I be for aye thy vassal blest?
Thy beauty's shield, heart-shaped and vermeil-dyed?
Ah, silver shrine, here will I take my rest
After so many hours of toil and quest,
A famished pilgrim,—saved by miracle.
Though I have found, I will not rob thy nest,
Saving of thy sweet self; if thou think'st well
To trust, fair Madeline, to no rude infidel.

39

"Hark! 'tis an elfin-storm from faery land,
Of haggard seeming, but a boon indeed:
Arise—arise! the morning is at hand;—
The bloated wassailers will never heed;—
Let us away, my love, with happy speed;
There are no ears to hear, or eyes to see,—
Drowned all in Rhenish and the sleepy mead:
Awake! arise! my love, and fearless be,
For o'er the southern moors I have a home for thee."

40

She hurried at his words, beset with fears,
For there were sleeping dragons all around,
At glaring watch, perhaps, with ready spears—
Down the wide stairs a darkling way they found;
In all the house was heard no human sound.
A chain-drooped lamp was flickering by each door;

The arras, rich with horseman, hawk, and hound,
Fluttered in the besieging wind's uproar;
And the long carpets rose along the gusty floor.

41

They glide, like phantoms, into the wide hall;
Like phantoms, to the iron porch they glide,
Where lay the Porter, in uneasy sprawl,
With a huge empty flagon by his side:
The wakeful bloodhound rose, and shook his hide,
But his sagacious eye an inmate owns:
By one, and one, the bolts full easy slide:—
The chains lie silent on the footworn stones;
The key turns, and the door upon its hinges groans.

42

And they are gone: aye, ages long ago
These lovers fled away into the storm.
That night the Baron dreamt of many a woe,
And all his warrior-guests with shade and form
Of witch, and demon, and large coffin-worm,
Were long be-nightmared. Angela the old
Died palsy-twitched, with meager face deform;
The Beadsman, after thousand aves told,
For aye unsought-for slept among his ashes cold.

74 GEORGE DARLEY

It Is Not Beauty I Demand

It is not Beauty I demand,
  A crystal brow, the moon's despair,
Nor the snow's daughter, a white hand,
  Nor mermaid's yellow pride of hair.

Tell me not of your starry eyes,
  Your lips that seem on roses fed,
Your breasts where Cupid trembling lies,
  Nor sleeps for kissing of his bed.

A bloomy pair of vermeil cheeks,
  Like Hebe's in her ruddiest hours,
A breath that softer music speaks
  Than summer winds a-wooing flowers.

These are but gauds; nay, what are lips?
  Coral beneath the ocean-stream,
Whose brink when your adventurer sips
  Full oft he perisheth on them.

And what are cheeks but ensigns oft
  That wave hot youth to fields of blood?
Did Helen's breast though ne'er so soft,
  Do Greece or Ilium any good?

Eyes can with baleful ardor burn,
  Poison can breath that erst perfumed,

There's many a white hand holds an urn
With lovers' hearts to dust consumed.

For crystal brows—there's naught within,
They are but empty cells for pride;
He who the Syren's hair would win
Is mostly strangled in the tide.

Give me, instead of beauty's bust,
A tender heart, a loyal mind,
Which with temptation I could trust.
Yet never linked with error find.

One in whose gentle bosom I
Could pour my secret heart of woes,
Like the care-burdened honey-fly
That hides his murmurs in the rose.

My earthly comforter! whose love
So indefeasible might be,
That when my spirit won above
Hers could not stay for sympathy.

75. THOMAS HOOD

The Song of the Shirt

With fingers weary and worn,
  With eyelids heavy and red,
A woman sat, in unwomanly rags,
  Plying her needle and thread,—
    Stitch! stitch! stitch!
In poverty, hunger, and dirt;
  And still with a voice of dolorous pitch
She sang the "Song of the Shirt!"

"Work! work! work
  While the cock is crowing aloof!
And work—work—work
  Till the stars shine through the roof!
It's, O, to be a slave
  Along with the barbarous Turk,
Where woman has never a soul to save,
  If this is Christian work!

"Work—work—work
  Till the brain begins to swim!
Work—work—work
  Till the eyes are heavy and dim!
Seam, and gusset, and band,
  Band, and gusset, and seam,—
Till over the buttons I fall asleep,
  And sew them on in a dream!

"O men with sisters dear!
O men with mothers and wives!
It is not linen you're wearing out,
But human creatures' lives!
Stitch—stitch—stitch,
In poverty, hunger, and dirt,—
Sewing at once, with a double thread,
A shroud as well as a shirt!

"But why do I talk of death,—
That phantom of grisly bone?
I hardly fear his terrible shape,
It seems so like my own,—
It seems so like my own
Because of the fasts I keep;
O God! that bread should be so dear,
And flesh and blood so cheap!

"Work—work—work!
My labor never flags;
And what are its wages? A bed of straw,
A crust of bread—and rags,
That shattered roof—and this naked floor—
A table—a broken chair—
And a wall so blank my shadow I thank
For sometimes falling there!

"Work—work—work
From weary chime to chime!
Work—work—work
As prisoners work for crime!

Band, and gusset, and seam,
  Seam, and gusset, and band,—
Till the heart is sick and the brain benumbed,
  As well as the weary hand.

"Work—work—work
  In the dull December light?
And work—work—work
  When the weather is warm and bright!
While underneath the eaves
  The brooding swallows cling,
As if to show me their sunny backs,
  And twit me with the Spring.

"O, but to breathe the breath
  Of the cowslip and primrose sweet,—
With the sky above my head,
  And the grass beneath my feet!
For only one short hour
  To feel as I used to feel,
Before I knew the woes of want
  And the walk that costs a meal!

"O, but for one short hour,—
  A respite, however brief!
No blessèd leisure for love or hope,
  But only time for grief!
A little weeping would ease my heart;
  But in their briny bed
My tears must stop, for every drop
  Hinders needle and thread!"

With fingers weary and worn,
  With eyelids heavy and red,
A woman sat, in unwomanly rags,
  Plying her needle and thread,—
    Stitch! stitch! stitch!
  In poverty, hunger, and dirt;
And still with a voice of dolorous pitch—
Would that its tone could reach the rich!—
  She sang this "Song of the Shirt!"

76 WINTHROP MACKWORTH PRAED

The Vicar

Some years ago, ere time and taste
  Had turn'd our parish topsy-turvy,
When Darnel Park was Darnel Waste,
  And roads as little known as scurvy,
The man who lost his way, between
  St. Mary's Hill and Sandy Thicket,
Was always shown across the green,
  And guided to the Parson's wicket.

Back flew the bolt of lissom lath;
  Fair Margaret, in her tidy kirtle,
Led the lorn traveller up the path,
  Through clean-clipt rows of box and myrtle;
And Don and Sancho, Tramp and Tray,
  Upon the parlour steps collected,
Wagg'd all their tails, and seem'd to say—
  'Our master knows you—you're expected.'

Uprose the Reverend Dr. Brown,
  Uprose the Doctor's winsome marrow;
The lady laid her knitting down,
  Her husband clasp'd his ponderous Barrow;
Whate'er the stranger's caste or creed,
  Pundit or Papist, saint or sinner,
He found a stable for his steed,
  And welcome for himself, and dinner.

If, when he reach'd his journey's end,
  And warm'd himself in Court or College,
He had not gained an honest friend
  And twenty curious scraps of knowledge,—
If he departed as he came,
  With no new light on love or liquor,—
Good sooth, the traveller was to blame,
  And not the Vicarage, nor the Vicar.

His talk was like a spring, which runs
  With rapid change from rocks to roses:
It slipped from politics to puns,
  It passed from Mahomet to Moses;
Beginning with the laws which keep
  The planets in their radiant courses,
And ending with some precept deep
  For dressing eels, or shoeing horses.

He was a shrewd and sound Divine,
  Of loud Dissent the mortal terror;
And when, by dint of page and line,
  He 'stablish'd Truth, or startled Error,
The Baptist found him far too deep;
  The Deist sigh'd with saving sorrow;
And the lean Levite went to sleep,
  And dream'd of tasting pork to-morrow.

His sermons never said or show'd
  That Earth is foul, that Heaven is gracious,
Without refreshment on the road
  From Jerome or from Athanasius:

And sure a righteous zeal inspired
  The hand and head that penn'd and plann'd them,
For all who understood admired,
  And some who did not understand them.

He wrote, too, in a quiet way,
  Small treatises, and smaller verses,
And sage remarks on chalk and clay,
  And hints to noble Lords—and nurses;
True histories of last year's ghost,
  Lines to a ringlet, or a turban,
And trifles for the *Morning Post*,
  And nothings for Sylvanus Urban.

He did not think all mischief fair,
  Although he had a knack of joking;
He did not make himself a bear,
  Although he had a taste for smoking;
And when religious sects ran mad,
  He held, in spite of all his learning,
That if a man's belief is bad,
  It will not be improved by burning.

And he was kind, and loved to sit
  In the low hut or garnish'd cottage,
And praise the farmer's homely wit,
  And share the widow's homelier pottage:
At his approach complaint grew mild;
  And when his hand unbarr'd the shutter,
The clammy lips of fever smiled
  The welcome which they could not utter.

He always had a tale for me
  Of Julius Caesar, or of Venus;
From him I learnt the rule of three,
  Cat's cradle, leap-frog, and *Quae genus:*
I used to singe his powder'd wig,
  To steal the staff he put such trust in,
And make the puppy dance a jig,
  When he began to quote Augustine.

Alack the change! in vain I look
  For haunts in which my boyhood trifled,—
The level lawn, the trickling brook,
  The trees I climb'd, the beds I rifled:
The church is larger than before;
  You reach it by a carriage entry;
It holds three hundred people more,
  And pews are fitted up for gentry.

Sit in the Vicar's seat: you'll hear
  The doctrine of a gentle Johnian,
Whose hand is white, whose tone is clear,
  Whose phrase is very Ciceronian.
Where is the old man laid?—look down,
  And construe on the slab before you,
'Hic jacet Gvlielmvs Brown,
  Vir nullâ non donandus lauru.'

77 JAMES CLARENCE MANGAN

The Nameless One

Roll forth, my song, like the rushing river,
 That sweeps along to the mighty sea;
God will inspire me while I deliver
  My soul of thee!

Tell thou the world, when my bones lie whitening
 Amid the last homes of youth and eld,
That once there was one whose veins ran lightning
  No eye beheld.

Tell how his boyhood was one drear night-hour,
 How shone for him, through his griefs and gloom,
No star of all heaven sends to light our
  Path to the tomb.

Roll on, my song, and to after ages
 Tell how, disdaining all earth can give,
He would have taught men, from wisdom's pages,
  The way to live.

And tell how trampled, derided, hated,
 And worn by weakness, disease, and wrong,
He fled for shelter to God, who mated
  His soul with song.

—With song which alway, sublime or vapid,
 Flow'd like a rill in the morning beam,

Perchance not deep, but intense and rapid—
A mountain stream.

Tell how this Nameless, condemn'd for years long
To herd with demons from hell beneath,
Saw things that made him, with groans and tears, long
For even death.

Go on to tell how, with genius wasted,
Betray'd in friendship, befool'd in love,
With spirit shipwreck'd, and young hopes blasted,
He still, still strove;

Till, spent with toil, dreeing death for others
(And some whose hands should have wrought for him,
If children live not for sires and mothers),
His mind grew dim;

And he fell far through that pit abysmal,
The gulf and grave of Maginn and Burns,
And pawn'd his soul for the devil's dismal
Stock of returns.

But yet redeem'd it in days of darkness,
And shapes and signs of the final wrath,
When death, in hideous and ghastly starkness,
Stood on his path.

And tell how now, amid wreck and sorrow,
And want, and sickness, and houseless nights,

He bides in calmness the silent morrow,
That no ray lights.

And lives he still, then? Yes! Old and hoary
At thirty-nine, from despair and woe,
He lives, enduring what future story
Will never know.

Him grant a grave to, ye pitying noble,
Deep in your bosoms: there let him dwell!
He, too, had tears for all souls in trouble,
Here and in hell.

78 THOMAS LOVELL BEDDOES

Song

Old Adam, the carrion crow,
  The old crow of Cairo;
He sat in the shower, and let it flow
  Under his tail and over his crest;
    And through every feather
    Leaked the wet weather;
  And the bough swung under his nest;
  For his beak it was heavy with marrow.
    Is that the wind dying? O no;
    It's only two devils, that blow
    Through a murderer's bones, to and fro,
      In the ghosts' moonshine.

Ho! Eve, my gray carrion wife,
  When we have supped on kings' marrow,
Where shall we drink and make merry our life?
  Our nest it is queen Cleopatra's skull,
    'Tis cloven and cracked,
    And battered and hacked,
  But with tears of blue eyes it is full:
  Let us drink then, my raven of Cairo.
    Is that the wind dying? O no;
    It's only two devils, that blow
    Through a murderer's bones, to and fro,
      In the ghosts' moonshine.

79 RALPH WALDO EMERSON

Brahma

If the red slayer think he slays,
  Or if the slain think he is slain,
They know not well the subtle ways
  I keep, and pass, and turn again.

Far or forgot to me is near;
  Shadow and sunlight are the same;
The vanish'd gods to me appear;
  And one to me are shame and fame.

They reckon ill who leave me out;
  When me they fly, I am the wings;
I am the doubter and the doubt,
  And I the hymn the Brahmin sings.

The strong gods pine for my abode,
  And pine in vain the sacred Seven;
But thou, meek lover of the good!
  Find me, and turn thy back on heaven.

The Bells of Shandon

With deep affection,
  And recollection,
I often think of
  Those Shandon bells,
Whose sounds so wild would,
In the days of childhood,
Fling around my cradle
  Their magic spells.

On this I ponder
Where'er I wander,
And thus grow fonder,
  Sweet Cork, of thee;
With thy bells of Shandon,
That sound so grand on
The pleasant waters
  Of the River Lee.

I've heard bells chiming
Full many a clime in,
Tolling sublime in
  Cathedral shrine,
While at a glib rate
Brass tongues would vibrate—
But all their music
  Spoke naught like thine;
For memory, dwelling

On each proud swelling
Of the belfry knelling
  Its bold notes free,
Made the bells of Shandon
Sound far more grand on
The pleasant waters
  Of the River Lee.

I've heard bells tolling
Old Adrian's Mole in,
Their thunder rolling
  From the Vatican,
And cymbals glorious
Swinging uproarious
In the gorgeous turrets
  Of Notre Dame;
But thy sounds were sweeter
Than the dome of Peter
Flings o'er the Tiber,
  Pealing solemnly—
O, the bells of Shandon
Sound far more grand on
The pleasant waters
  Of the River Lee.

There's a bell in Moscow,
While on tower and kiosk O!
In Saint Sophia
  The Turkman gets,
And loud in air
Calls men to prayer

From the tapering summits
  Of tall minarets.
Such empty phantom
I freely grant them;
But there's an anthem
  More dear to me,—
'Tis the bells of Shandon,
That sound so grand on
The pleasant waters
  Of the River Lee.

81 ELIZABETH BARRETT BROWNING

Sonnets from the Portuguese (v)

When our two souls stand up erect and strong,
  Face to face, silent, drawing nigh and nigher,
  Until the lengthening wings break into fire
At either curving point,—what bitter wrong
Can the earth do us, that we should not long
  Be here contented? Think! In mounting higher,
  The angels would press on us, and aspire
To drop some golden orb of perfect song
Into our deep, dear silence. Let us stay
  Rather on earth, Belovèd—where the unfit
Contrarious moods of men recoil away
  And isolate pure spirits, and permit
A place to stand and love in for a day,
  With darkness and the death-hour rounding it.

82 JOHN GREENLEAF WHITTIER

The Barefoot Boy

Blessings on thee, little man,
Barefoot boy, with cheek of tan!
With thy turned-up pantaloons,
And thy merry whistled tunes;
With thy red lip, redder still
Kissed by strawberries on the hill;
With the sunshine on thy face,
Through thy torn brim's jaunty grace;
From my heart I give thee joy,—
I was once a barefoot boy!
Prince thou art,—the grown-up man
Only is republican.
Let the million-dollared ride!
Barefoot, trudging at his side,
Thou hast more than he can buy
In the reach of ear and eye,—
Outward sunshine, inward joy:
Blessings on thee, barefoot boy!

Oh for boyhood's painless play,
Sleep that wakes in laughing day,
Health that mocks the doctor's rules,
Knowledge never learned of schools,
Of the wild bee's morning chase,
Of the wild-flower's time and place,
Flight of fowl and habitude

Of the tenants of the wood:
How the tortoise bears his shell,
How the woodchuck digs his cell,
And the ground-mole sinks his well;
How the robin feeds her young,
How the oriole's nest is hung;
Where the whitest lilies blow,
Where the freshest berries grow,
Where the ground-nut trails its vine,
Where the wood-grape's clusters shine;
Of the black wasp's cunning way,
Mason of his walls of clay,
And the architectural plans
Of gray hornet artisans!
For, eschewing books and tasks,
Nature answers all he asks;
Hand in hand with her he walks,
Face to face with her he talks,
Part and parcel of her joy,—
Blessings on the barefoot boy!

Oh for boyhood's time of June,
Crowding years in one brief moon,
When all things I heard or saw,
Me, their master, waited for.
I was rich in flowers and trees,
Humming-birds and honey-bees;
For my sport the squirrel played,
Plied the snouted mole his spade;
For my taste the blackberry cone
Purpled over hedge and stone;

Laughed the brook for my delight
Through the day and through the night,
Whispering at the garden wall,
Talked with me from fall to fall;
Mine the sand-rimmed pickerel pond,
Mine the walnut slopes beyond,
Mine, on bending orchard trees,
Apples of Hesperides!
Still as my horizon grew,
Larger grew my riches too;
All the world I saw or knew
Seemed a complex Chinese toy,
Fashioned for a barefoot boy!
Oh for festal dainties spread,
Like my bowl of milk and bread;
Pewter spoon and bowl of wood,
On the door-stone, gray and rude!
O'er me, like a regal tent,
Cloudy-ribbed, the sunset bent,
Purple-curtained, fringed with gold,
Looped in many a wind-swung fold;
While for music came the play
Of the pied frogs' orchestra;
And, to light the noisy choir,
Lit the fly his lamp of fire.
I was monarch: pomp and joy
Waited on the barefoot boy!

Cheerily, then, my little man,
Live and laugh, as boyhood can!
Though the flinty slopes be hard,

Stubble-speared the new-mown sward,
Every morn shall lead thee through
Fresh baptisms of the dew:
Every evening from thy feet
Shall the cool wind kiss the heat:
All too soon these feet must hide
In the prison cells of pride,
Lose the freedom of the sod,
Like a colt's for work be shod,
Made to tread the mills of toil,
Up and down in ceaseless moil:
Happy if their track be found
Never on forbidden ground;
Happy if they sink not in
Quick and treacherous sands of sin.
Ah! that thou couldst know thy joy,
Ere it passes, barefoot boy!

83 HENRY WADSWORTH LONGFELLOW

The Children's Hour

Between the dark and the daylight,
  When the night is beginning to lower,
Comes a pause in the day's occupations,
  That is known as the Children's Hour.

I hear in the chamber above me
  The patter of little feet,
The sound of a door that is opened,
  And voices soft and sweet.

From my study I see in the lamplight,
  Descending the broad hall stair,
Grave Alice, and laughing Allegra,
  And Edith with golden hair.

A whisper, and then a silence:
  Yet I know by their merry eyes
They are plotting and planning together
  To take me by surprise.

A sudden rush from the stairway,
  A sudden raid from the hall!
By three doors left unguarded
  They enter my castle wall!

They climb up into my turret
  O'er the arms and back of my chair;

If I try to escape, they surround me;
  They seem to be everywhere.

They almost devour me with kisses,
  Their arms about me entwine,
Till I think of the Bishop of Bingen
  In his Mouse-Tower on the Rhine!

Do you think, O blue-eyed banditti,
  Because you have scaled the wall,
Such an old mustache as I am
  Is not a match for you all!

I have you fast in my fortress,
  And will not let you depart,
But put you down into the dungeon
  In the round-tower of my heart.

And there will I keep you forever,
  Yes, forever and a day,
Till the walls shall crumble to ruin,
  And moulder in dust away!

The Raven

Once upon a midnight dreary, while I pondered, weak
 and weary,
Over many a quaint and curious volume of forgotten lore—
While I nodded, nearly napping, suddenly there came a
 tapping,
As of some one gently rapping, rapping at my chamber
 door.
" 'Tis some visitor," I muttered, "tapping at my
 chamber door—
 Only this and nothing more."

Ah, distinctly I remember it was in the bleak December,
And each separate dying ember wrought its ghost upon
 the floor.
Eagerly I wished the morrow;—vainly I had sought to
 borrow
From my books surcease of sorrow—sorrow for the lost
 Lenore—
For the rare and radiant maiden whom the angels name
 Lenore—
 Nameless *here* for evermore.

And the silken sad uncertain rustling of each purple
 curtain
Thrilled me—filled me with fantastic terrors never felt
 before;

So that now, to still the beating of my heart, I stood
repeating:
" 'Tis some visitor entreating entrance at my chamber
door—
Some late visitor entreating entrance at my chamber door;
This it is and nothing more."

Presently my soul grew stronger; hesitating then no longer,
"Sir," said I, "or Madam, truly your forgiveness I implore;
But the fact is I was napping, and so gently you came
rapping,
And so faintly you came tapping, tapping at my
chamber door,
That I scarce was sure I heard you"—here I opened
wide the door;—
Darkness there and nothing more.

Deep into that darkness peering, long I stood there,
wondering, fearing,
Doubting, dreaming dreams no mortal ever dared to
dream before;
But the silence was unbroken, and the stillness gave no
token,
And the only word there spoken was the whispered
word "Lenore!"
This I whispered, and an echo murmured back the
word "Lenore!"
Merely this and nothing more.

Back into the chamber turning, all my soul within me
burning,

Soon again I heard a tapping, something louder than
before.
"Surely," said I, "surely that is something at my window
lattice;
Let me see, then, what thereat is, and this mystery
explore,—
Let my heart be still a moment, and this mystery
explore,—
'Tis the wind and nothing more."

Open here I flung the shutter, when, with many a flirt
and flutter,
In there stepped a stately Raven of the saintly days of yore.
Not the least obeisance made he, not a minute stopped
or stayed he,
But with mien of lord or lady perched above my
chamber door—
Perched upon a bust of Pallas just above my chamber
door—
Perched, and sat, and nothing more.

Then, this ebony bird beguiling my sad fancy into smiling,
By the grave and stern decorum of the countenance it
wore,
"Though thy crest be shorn and shaven, thou," I said,
"art sure no craven,
Ghastly, grim and ancient Raven, wandering from the
nightly shore:
Tell me what thy lordly name is on the night's Plutonian
shore!"
Quoth the Raven, "Nevermore."

Much I marvelled this ungainly fowl to hear discourse
so plainly,
Though its answer little meaning, little relevancy bore;
For we cannot help agreeing that no living human being
Ever yet was blessed with seeing bird above his
chamber door—
Bird or beast upon the sculptured bust above his
chamber door—
With such name as "Nevermore."

But the Raven, sitting lonely on that placid bust, spoke
only
That one word, as if his soul in that one word he did
outpour.
Nothing farther then he uttered, not a feather then he
fluttered;
Till I scarcely more than muttered, "Other friends have
flown before:
On the morrow *he* will leave me, as my hopes have flown
before."
Then the bird said, "Nevermore."

Startled at the stillness broken by reply so aptly spoken,
"Doubtless," said I, "what it utters is its only stock and
store,
Caught from some unhappy master whom unmerciful
Disaster
Followed fast and followed faster till his songs one
burden bore,
Till the dirges of his hope that melancholy burden bore
Of 'Never—nevermore.' "

But the Raven still beguiling all my sad fancy into smiling,
Straight I wheeled a cushioned seat in front of bird and
bust and door;
Then, upon the velvet sinking, I betook myself to linking
Fancy unto fancy, thinking what this ominous bird of
yore,
What this grim, ungainly, ghastly, gaunt, and ominous
bird of yore
Meant in croaking "Nevermore."

This I sat engaged in guessing, but no syllable expressing
To the fowl, whose fiery eyes now burned into my
bosom's core;
This and more I sat divining, with my head at ease reclining
On the cushion's velvet lining that the lamplight
gloated o'er,
But whose velvet violet lining with the lamplight
gloating o'er,
She shall press, ah, nevermore!

Then, methought, the air grew denser, perfumed from
an unseen censer
Swung by Seraphim whose foot-falls tinkled on the
tufted floor.
"Wretch," I cried, "thy God hath lent thee—by these
angels he hath sent thee
Respite—respite and nepenthe, from thy memories of
Lenore!
Quaff, oh quaff this kind nepenthe, and forget this lost
Lenore!"
Quoth the Raven, "Nevermore."

"Prophet!" said I, "thing of evil! prophet still, if bird
or devil!
Whether Tempter sent, or whether tempest tossed thee
here ashore,
Desolate yet all undaunted, on this desert land
enchanted—
On this home by Horror haunted,—tell me truly, I
implore:
Is there—*is* there balm in Gilead?—tell me—tell me, I
implore!"
Quoth the Raven, "Nevermore."

"Prophet!" said I, "thing of evil!—prophet still, if bird
or devil!
By that Heaven that bends above us, by that God we
both adore:
Tell this soul with sorrow laden if, within the distant
Aidenn,
It shall clasp a sainted maiden whom the angels name
Lenore:
Clasp a rare and radiant maiden whom the angels name
Lenore:"
Quoth the Raven, "Nevermore."

"Be that word our sign of parting, bird or fiend!" I
shrieked, upstarting:
"Get thee back into the tempest and the night's
Plutonian shore!
Leave no black plume as a token of that lie thy soul hath
spoken!

Leave my loneliness unbroken!—quit the bust above
my door!
Take thy beak from out my heart, and take thy form
from off my door!"
Quoth the Raven, "Nevermore."

And the Raven, never flitting, still is sitting, still is
sitting
On the pallid bust of Pallas just above my chamber
door;
And his eyes have all the seeming of a demon's that is
dreaming,
And the lamplight o'er him streaming throws his
shadow on the floor;
And my soul from out that shadow that lies floating on
the floor
Shall be lifted—nevermore!

84 EDWARD FITZGERALD

FROM *The Rubaiyat of Omar Khayyam*

XCVI

Yet Ah, that Spring should vanish with the Rose!
That Youth's sweet-scented manuscript should close!
  The Nightingale that in the branches sang,
Ah whence, and whither flown again, who knows?

XCVII

Would but the Desert of the Fountain yield
One glimpse—if dimly, yet indeed, reveal'd,
  To which the fainting Traveler might spring,
As springs the trampled herbage of the field!

XCVIII

Would but some winged Angel ere too late
Arrest the yet unfolded Roll of Fate,
  And make the stern Recorder otherwise
Enregister, or quite obliterate!

XCIX

Ah Love! could you and I with Him conspire
To grasp this sorry Scheme of Things entire,
  Would not we shatter it to bits—and then
Re-mould it nearer to the Heart's Desire!

C

Yon rising Moon that looks for us again—
How oft hereafter will she wax and wane;
  How oft hereafter rising look for us
Through this same Garden—and for *one* in vain!

CI

And when like her, oh Saki, you shall pass
Among the Guests Star-scatter'd on the Grass,
  And in your joyous errand reach the spot
Where I made One—turn down an empty Glass!

86 ALFRED, LORD TENNYSON

Song of the Lotos-Eaters

There is sweet music here that softer falls
Than petals from blown roses on the grass,
Or night-dews on still waters between walls
Of shadowy granite, in a gleaming pass;
Music that gentlier on the spirit lies,
Than tired eyelids upon tired eyes;
Music that brings sweet sleep down from the
blissful skies.
Here are cool mosses deep,
And thro' the moss the ivies creep,
And in the stream the long-leaved flowers weep,
And from the craggy ledge the poppy hangs in sleep.

Why are we weigh'd upon with heaviness,
And utterly consumed with sharp distress,
While all things else have rest from weariness?
All things have rest: why should we toil alone,
We only toil, who are the first of things,
And make perpetual moan,
Still from one sorrow to another thrown:
Nor ever fold our wings,
And cease from wanderings,
Nor steep our brows in slumber's holy balm;
Nor harken what the inner spirit sings,
'There is no joy but calm!'—
Why should we only toil, the roof and crown
of things?

Lo! in the middle of the wood,
The folded leaf is woo'd from out the bud
With winds upon the branch, and there
Grows green and broad, and takes no care,
Sun-steep'd at noon, and in the moon
Nightly dew-fed; and turning yellow
Falls, and floats adown the air.
Lo! sweeten'd with the summer light,
The full-juiced apple, waxing over-mellow,
Drops in a silent autumn night.
All its allotted length of days,
The flower ripens in its place,
Ripens and fades, and falls, and hath no toil,
Fast-rooted in the fruitful soil.

Hateful is the dark-blue sky,
Vaulted o'er the dark-blue sea.
Death is the end of life; ah, why
Should life all labour be?
Let us alone. Time driveth onward fast,
And in a little while our lips are dumb.
Let us alone. What is it that will last?
All things are taken from us, and become
Portions and parcels of the dreadful Past.
Let us alone. What pleasure can we have
To war with evil? Is there any peace
In ever climbing up the climbing wave?
All things have rest, and ripen toward the grave
In silence; ripen, fall and cease:
Give us long rest or death, dark death,
or dreamful ease.

How sweet it were, hearing the downward stream,
With half-shut eyes ever to seem
Falling asleep in a half-dream!
To dream and dream, like yonder amber light,
Which will not leave the myrrh-bush on the height;
To hear each other's whisper'd speech;
Eating the Lotus day by day,
To watch the crisping ripples on the beach,
And tender curving lines of creamy spray;
To lend our hearts and spirits wholly
To the influence of mild-minded melancholy;
To muse and brood and live again in memory,
With those old faces of our infancy
Heap'd over with a mound of grass,
Two handfuls of white dust, shut in an urn of brass!

Dear is the memory of our wedded lives,
And dear the last embraces of our wives
And their warm tears: but all hath suffer'd change;
For surely now our household hearths are cold:
Our sons inherit us: our looks are strange:
And we should come like ghosts to trouble joy.
Or else the island princes over-bold
Have eat our substance, and the minstrel sings
Before them of the ten years' war in Troy,
And our great deeds, as half-forgotten things.
Is there confusion in the little isle?
Let what is broken so remain.
The Gods are hard to reconcile:
'Tis hard to settle order once again.
There *is* confusion worse than death,

Trouble on trouble, pain on pain,
Long labour unto aged breath,
Sore task to hearts worn out with many wars
And eyes grown dim with gazing on the pilot-stars.

But propt on beds of amaranth and moly,
How sweet (while warm airs lull us, blowing lowly)
With half-dropt eyelids still,
Beneath a heaven dark and holy,
To watch the long bright river drawing slowly
His waters from the purple hill—
To hear the dewy echoes calling
From cave to cave thro' the thick-twinèd vine—
To watch the emerald-colour'd water falling
Thro' many a wov'n acanthus-wreath divine!
Only to hear and see the far-off sparkling brine,
Only to hear were sweet, stretch'd out beneath the pine.

The Lotos blooms below the barren peak:
The Lotos blows by every winding creek:
All day the wind breathes low with mellower tone:
Thro' every hollow cave and alley lone
Round and round the spicy downs the yellow Lotos-dust is
blown.
We have had enough of action, and of motion we,
Roll'd to starboard, roll'd to larboard, when the surge was
seething free,
Where the wallowing monster spouted his foam-fountains
in the sea.
Let us swear an oath, and keep it with an equal mind,
In the hollow Lotos-land to live and lie reclined

On the hills like Gods together, careless of mankind.
For they lie beside their nectar, and the bolts are hurl'd
Far below them in the valleys, and the clouds are lightly curl'd
Round their golden houses, girdled with the gleaming world:
Where they smile in secret, looking over wasted lands,
Blight and famine, plague and earthquake, roaring deeps and fiery sands,
Clanging fights, and flaming towns, and sinking ships, and praying hands.
But they smile, they find a music centred in a doleful song
Steaming up, a lamentation and an ancient tale of wrong,
Like a tale of little meaning tho' the words are strong;
Chanted from an ill-used race of men that cleave the soil,
Sow the seed, and reap the harvest with enduring toil,
Storing yearly little dues of wheat, and wine and oil;
Till they perish and they suffer—some, 'tis whisper'd—down in hell
Suffer endless anguish, others in Elysian valleys dwell,
Resting weary limbs at last on beds of asphodel.
Surely, surely, slumber is more sweet than toil, the shore
Than labour in the deep mid-ocean, wind and wave and oar;
O rest ye, brother mariners, we will not wander more.

87 ROBERT BROWNING

My Last Duchess

FERRARA

That's my last Duchess painted on the wall,
Looking as if she were alive. I call
That piece a wonder, now: Fra Pandolf's hands
Worked busily a day, and there she stands.
Will't please you sit and look at her? I said
"Fra Pandolf" by design, for never read
Strangers like you that pictured countenance,
The depth and passion of its earnest glance,
But to myself they turned (since none puts by
The curtain I have drawn for you, but I)
And seemed as they would ask me, if they durst,
How such a glance came there; so, not the first
Are you to turn and ask thus. Sir, 'twas not
Her husband's presence only, called that spot
Of joy into the Duchess' cheek: perhaps
Fra Pandolf chanced to say, "Her mantle laps
Over my lady's wrist too much," or "Paint
Must never hope to reproduce the faint
Half-flush that dies along her throat:" such stuff
Was courtesy, she thought, and cause enough
For calling up that spot of joy. She had
A heart—how shall I say?—too soon made glad,
Too easily impressed: she liked whate'er
She looked on, and her looks went everywhere.
Sir, 'twas all one! My favour at her breast,

The dropping of the daylight in the West,
The bough of cherries some officious fool
Broke in the orchard for her, the white mule
She rode with round the terrace—all and each
Would draw from her alike the approving speech,
Or blush, at least. She thanked men,—good! but thanked
Somehow—I know not how—as if she ranked
My gift of a nine-hundred-years-old name
With anybody's gift. Who'd stoop to blame
This sort of trifling? Even had you skill
In speech—(which I have not)—to make your will
Quite clear to such an one, and say, "Just this
Or that in you disgusts me; here you miss,
Or there exceed the mark"—and if she let
Herself be lessoned so, nor plainly set
Her wits to yours, forsooth, and made excuse,
—E'en then would be some stooping; and I choose
Never to stoop. Oh sir, she smiled, no doubt,
Whene'er I passed her; but who passed without
Much the same smile? This grew; I gave commands;
Then all smiles stopped together. There she stands
As if alive. Will't please you rise? We'll meet
The company below, then. I repeat,
The Count your master's known munificence
Is ample warrant that no just pretence
Of mine for dowry will be disallowed;
Though his fair daughter's self, as I avowed
At starting, is my object. Nay, we'll go
Together down, sir. Notice Neptune, though,
Taming a sea-horse, thought a rarity,
Which Claus of Innsbruck cast in bronze for me!

The Owl and the Pussy-cat

The Owl and the Pussy-cat went to sea
  In a beautiful pea-green boat:
They took some honey, and plenty of money
  Wrapped up in a five-pound note.
The Owl looked up to the stars above,
  And sang to a small guitar,
"O lovely Pussy, O Pussy, my love,
  What a beautiful Pussy you are,
      You are,
      You are!
  What a beautiful Pussy you are!"

Pussy said to the Owl, "You elegant fowl,
  How charmingly sweet you sing!
Oh! let us be married; too long we have tarried:
  But what shall we do for a ring?"
They sailed away, for a year and a day,
  To the land where the bong-tree grows;
And there in a wood a Piggy-wig stood,
  With a ring at the end of his nose,
      His nose,
      His nose,
  With a ring at the end of his nose.

"Dear Pig, are you willing to sell for one shilling
  Your ring?" Said the Piggy, "I will."
So they took it away, and were married next day

By the turkey who lives on the hill.
They dined on mince and slices of quince,
Which they ate with a runcible spoon;
And hand in hand, on the edge of the sand,
They danced by the light of the moon,
The moon,
The moon,
They danced by the light of the moon.

89 HENRY DAVID THOREAU

'I Am a Parcel of Vain Strivings'

I am a parcel of vain strivings tied
By a chance bond together,
Dangling this way and that, their links
Were made so loose and wide,
Methinks,
For milder weather.

A bunch of violets without their roots,
And sorrel intermixed,
Encircled by a wisp of straw
Once coiled about their shoots,
The law
By which I'm fixed.

A nosegay which Time clutched from out
Those fair Elysian fields,
With weeds and broken stems, in haste,
Doth make the rabble rout
That waste
The day he yields.

And here I bloom for a short hour unseen,
Drinking my juices up,
With no root in the land
To keep my branches green,
But stand
In a bare cup.

Some tender buds were left upon my stem
In mimicry of life,
But ah! the children will not know,
Till time has withered them,
The woe
With which they're rife.

But now I see I was not plucked for naught,
And after in life's vase
Of glass set while I might survive,
But by a kind hand brought
Alive
To a strange place.

That stock thus thinned will soon redeem its hours,
And by another year,
Such as God knows, with freer air,
More fruits and fairer flowers
Will bear,
While I droop here.

Remembrance

Cold in the earth—and the deep snow piled above thee,
Far, far, removed, cold in the dreary grave!
Have I forgot, my only Love, to love thee,
Severed at last by Time's all-severing wave?

Now, when alone, do my thoughts no longer hover
Over the mountains, on that northern shore,
Resting their wings where heath and fern-leaves cover
That noble heart for ever, ever more?

Cold in the earth, and fifteen wild Decembers
From those brown hills have melted into spring:
Faithful, indeed, is the spirit that remembers
After such years of change and suffering!

Sweet Love of youth, forgive, if I forget thee,
While the world's tide is bearing me along;
Other desires and other hopes beset me,
Hopes which obscure, but cannot do thee wrong!

No later light has lightened up my heaven,
No second morn has ever shone for me;
All my life's bliss from thy dear life was given,
All my life's bliss is in the grave with thee.

But, when the days of golden dreams had perished,
And even Despair was powerless to destroy;

Then did I learn how existence could be cherished,
Strengthened, and fed without the aid of joy.

Then did I check the tears of useless passion—
Weaned my young soul from yearning after thine;
Sternly denied its burning wish to hasten
Down to that tomb already more than mine.

And, even yet, I dare not let it languish,
Dare not indulge in memory's rapturous pain;
Once drinking deep of that divinest anguish,
How could I seek the empty world again?

91 CHARLES KINGSLEY

The Three Fishers

Three fishers went sailing out into the west,—
  Out into the west as the sun went down;
Each thought of the woman who loved him the best,
  And the children stood watching them out of the town;
For men must work, and women must weep;
And there's little to earn, and many to keep,
    Though the harbor bar be moaning.

Three wives sat up in the light-house tower,
  And trimmed the lamps as the sun went down;
And they looked at the squall, and they looked at the shower,
  And the rack it came rolling up, ragged and brown;
But men must work, and women must weep,
Though storms be sudden, and waters deep,
    And the harbor bar be moaning.

Three corpses lay out on the shining sands
  In the morning gleam as the tide went down,
And the women are watching and wringing their hands,
  For those who will never come back to the town;
For men must work, and women must weep,—
And the sooner it's over, the sooner to sleep,—
    And good-by to the bar and its moaning.

92 ARTHUR HUGH CLOUGH

Say Not the Struggle Naught Availeth

Say not the struggle naught availeth,
  The labour and the wounds are vain,
The enemy faints not, nor faileth,
  And as things have been they remain.

If hopes were dupes, fears may be liars;
  It may be, in yon smoke conceal'd,
Your comrades chase e'en now the fliers,
  And, but for you, possess the field.

For while the tired waves, vainly breaking,
  Seem here no painful inch to gain,
Far back, through creeks and inlets making,
  Comes silent, flooding in, the main.

And not by eastern windows only,
  When daylight comes, comes in the light;
In front the sun climbs slow, how slowly!
  But westward, look, the land is bright!

93 WALT WHITMAN

The Last Invocation

At the last, tenderly,
From the walls of the powerful fortress'd house,
From the clasp of the knitted locks, from the keep
of the well-closed doors,
Let me be wafted.

Let me glide noiselessly forth;
With the key of softness unlock the locks—
with a whisper,
Set ope the doors O soul.

Tenderly—be not impatient,
(Strong is your hold O mortal flesh.
Strong is your hold O love.)

Dover Beach

The sea is calm to-night.
The tide is full, the moon lies fair
Upon the Straits;—on the French coast, the light
Gleams, and is gone; the cliffs of England stand,
Glimmering and vast, out in the tranquil bay.
Come to the window, sweet is the night air!
Only, from the long line of spray

Where the ebb meets the moon-blanch'd sand,
Listen! you hear the grating roar
Of pebbles which the waves suck back, and fling,
At their return, up the high strand,
Begin, and cease, and then again begin,
With tremulous cadence slow, and bring
The eternal note of sadness in.

Sophocles long ago
Heard it on the Ægæan, and it brought
Into his mind the turbid ebb and flow
Of human misery; we
Find also in the sound a thought,
Hearing it by this distant northern sea.

The sea of faith
Was once, too, at the full, and round earth's shore
Lay like the folds of a bright girdle furl'd;
But now I only hear

Its melancholy, long, withdrawing roar,
Retreating to the breath
Of the night-wind down the vast edges drear
And naked shingles of the world.

Ah, love, let us be true
To one another! for the world, which seems
To lie before us like a land of dreams,
So various, so beautiful, so new,
Hath really neither joy, nor love, nor light,
Nor certitude, nor peace, nor help for pain;
And we are here as on a darkling plain
Swept with confused alarms of struggle and flight,
Where ignorant armies clash by night.

95 GEORGE MEREDITH

Lucifer in Starlight

On a starr'd night Prince Lucifer uprose.
  Tired of his dark dominion swung the fiend
  Above the rolling ball in cloud part screen'd,
Where sinners hugg'd their spectre of repose.
Poor prey to his hot fit of pride were those.
  And now upon his western wing he lean'd,
  Now his huge bulk o'er Afric's sands careen'd,
Now the black planet shadow'd Arctic snows.
Soaring through wider zones that prick'd his scars
  With memory of the old revolt from Awe,
He reach'd a middle height, and at the stars,
Which are the brain of heaven, he look'd, and sank.
Around the ancient track march'd, rank on rank,
  The army of unalterable law.

The Choice

Think thou and act; to-morrow thou shalt die.
  Outstretch'd in the sun's warmth upon the shore,
  Thou say'st: 'Man's measured path is all gone o'er:
Up all his years, steeply, with strain and sigh,
Man clomb until he touch'd the truth; and I,
  Even I, am he whom it was destined for.'
  How should this be? Art thou then so much more
Than they who sow'd, that thou shouldst reap thereby?

Nay, come up hither. From this wave-wash'd mound
  Unto the furthest flood-brim look with me;
Then reach on with thy thought till it be drown'd.
  Miles and miles distant though the last line be,
And though thy soul sail leagues and leagues beyond,—
  Still, leagues beyond those leagues, there is more sea.

97 CHRISTINA GEORGINA ROSSETTI

Song

When I am dead, my dearest,
  Sing no sad songs for me;
Plant thou no roses at my head,
  Nor shady cypress tree:
Be the green grass above me
  With showers and dewdrops wet;
And if thou wilt, remember,
  And if thou wilt, forget.

I shall not see the shadows,
  I shall not feel the rain;
I shall not hear the nightingale
  Sing on, as if in pain;
And dreaming through the twilight
  That doth not rise nor set,
Haply I may remember,
  And haply may forget.

98 EMILY DICKINSON

After Great Pain . . . .

After great pain a formal feeling comes—
The nerves sit ceremonious like tombs;
The stiff Heart questions—was it He that bore?
And yesterday—or centuries before?

The feet mechanical
Go round a wooden way
Of ground or air or Ought, regardless grown,
A quartz contentment like a stone.

This is the hour of lead
Remembered if outlived,
As freezing persons recollect the snow—
First chill, then stupor, then the letting go.

99 LEWIS CARROLL

Father William

"You are old, Father William," the young man said,
  "And your hair has become very white;
And yet you incessantly stand on your head—
  Do you think, at your age, it is right?"

"In my youth," Father William replied to his son,
  "I feared it might injure the brain;
But, now that I'm perfectly sure I have none,
  Why, I do it again and again."

"You are old," said the youth, "as I mentioned before,
  And have grown most uncommonly fat;
Yet you turned a back-somersault in at the door—
  Pray, what is the reason of that?"

"In my youth," said the sage, as he shook his gray locks,
  "I kept all my limbs very supple
By the use of this ointment—one shilling the box—
  Allow me to sell you a couple?"

"You are old," said the youth, "and your jaws are too weak
  For anything tougher than suet;
Yet you finished the goose, with the bones and the beak—
  Pray, how did you manage to do it?"

"In my youth," said his father, "I took to the law,
  And argued each case with my wife;

And the muscular strength which it gave to my jaw,
  Has lasted the rest of my life."

"You are old," said the youth, "one would hardly suppose
  That your eye was as steady as ever;
Yet you balanced an eel on the end of your nose—
  What made you so awfully clever?"

"I have answered three questions, and that is enough,"
  Said his father; "don't give yourself airs!
Do you think I can listen all day to such stuff?
  Be off, or I'll kick you downstairs."

100 BRET HARTE

What the Bullet Sang

O joy of creation,
            To be!
O rapture, to fly
            And be free!
Be the battle lost or won,
Though its smoke shall hide the sun,
I shall find my love—the one
            Born for me!

I shall know him where he stands
            All alone,
With the power in his hands
            Not o'erthrown;
I shall know him by his face,
By his godlike front and grace;
I shall hold him for a space
            All my own!

It is he—O my love!
            So bold!
It is I—all thy love
            Foretold!
It is I—O love, what bliss!
Dost thou answer to my kiss?
O sweetheart! what is this
            Lieth there so cold?

101 THOMAS BAILEY ALDRICH

Memory

My mind lets go a thousand things,
Like dates of wars and deaths of kings,
And yet recalls the very hour—
'Twas noon by yonder village tower,
And on the last blue noon in May—
The wind came briskly up this way,
Crisping the brook beside the road;
Then, pausing here, set down its load
Of pine-scents, and shook listlessly
Two petals from that wild-rose tree.

102 ALGERNON CHARLES SWINBURNE

A Match

If love were what the rose is,
  And I were like the leaf,
Our lives would grow together
In sad or singing weather,
Blown fields or flowerful closes,
  Green pleasure or gray grief;
If love were what the rose is,
  And I were like the leaf.

If I were what the words are,
  And love were like the tune,
With double sound and single
Delight our lips would mingle,
With kisses glad as birds are
  That get sweet rain at noon;
If I were what the words are,
  And love were like the tune.

If you were life, my darling,
  And I, your love, were death,
We'd shine and snow together
Ere March made sweet the weather
With daffodil and starling
  And hours of fruitful breath;
If you were life, my darling,
  And I, your love, were death.

If you were thrall to sorrow,
  And I were page to joy,
We'd play for lives and seasons,
With loving looks and treasons,
And tears of night and morrow,
  And laughs of maid and boy;
If you were thrall to sorrow,
  And I were page to joy.

If you were April's lady,
  And I were lord in May,
We'd throw with leaves for hours,
And draw for days with flowers,
Till day like night were shady,
  And night were bright like day;
If you were April's lady,
  And I were lord in May.

If you were queen of pleasure,
  And I were king of pain,
We'd hunt down love together,
Pluck out his flying-feather,
And teach his feet a measure,
  And find his mouth a rein;
If you were queen of pleasure,
  And I were king of pain.

103 THOMAS HARDY

The Darkling Thrush

I leant upon a coppice gate
  When Frost was spectre-gray,
And Winter's dregs made desolate
  The weakening eye of day.
The tangled bine-stems scored the sky
  Like strings of broken lyres,
And all mankind that haunted nigh
  Had sought their household fires.

The land's sharp features seem'd to be
  The Century's corpse outleant,
His crypt the cloudy canopy,
  The wind his death-lament.
The ancient pulse of germ and birth
  Was shrunken hard and dry,
And every spirit upon earth
  Seem'd fervourless as I.

At once a voice arose among
  The bleak twigs overhead
In a full-hearted evensong
  Of joy illimited;
An aged thrush, frail, gaunt, and small,
  In blast-beruffled plume,
Had chosen thus to fling his soul
  Upon the growing gloom.

So little cause for carollings
   Of such ecstatic sound
Was written on terrestrial things
   Afar or nigh around,
That I could think there trembled through
   His happy good-night air
Some blessed Hope, whereof he knew
   And I was unaware.

104 GERARD MANLEY HOPKINS

Pied Beauty

Glory be to God for dappled things—
For skies of couple-colour as a brinded cow;
For rose-moles all in stipple upon trout that swim;
Fresh-firecoal chestnut-falls; finches' wings;
Landscape plotted and pieced—fold, fallow,
and plough;
And all trades, their gear and tackle and trim.

All things counter, original, spare, strange;
Whatever is fickle, freckled (who knows how?)
With swift, slow; sweet, sour; adazzle, dim;
He fathers-forth whose beauty is past change:
Praise him.

105 ROBERT BRIDGES

Nightingales

Beautiful must be the mountains whence ye come,
And bright in the fruitful valleys the streams, wherefrom
          Ye learn your song:
Where are those starry woods? O might I wander there,
   Among the flowers, which in that heavenly air
          Bloom the year long!

   Nay, barren are those mountains and spent the streams:
   Our song is the voice of desire, that haunts our dreams,
          A throe of the heart,
Whose pining visions dim, forbidden hopes profound,
   No dying cadence nor long sigh can sound,
          For all our art.

   Alone, aloud in the raptured ear of men
   We pour our dark nocturnal secret; and then,
          As night is withdrawn
From these sweet-springing meads and bursting boughs of
          May,
   Dream, while the innumerable choir of day
          Welcome the dawn.

106 WILLIAM ERNEST HENLEY

Invictus

Out of the night that covers me,
   Black as the pit from pole to pole,
I thank whatever gods may be
   For my unconquerable soul.

In the fell clutch of circumstance
   I have not winced nor cried aloud.
Under the bludgeonings of chance
   My head is bloody, but unbow'd.

Beyond this place of wrath and tears
   Looms but the Horror of the shade,
And yet the menace of the years
   Finds and shall find me unafraid.

It matters not how strait the gate,
   How charged with punishments the scroll,
I am the master of my fate:
   I am the captain of my soul.

107 ROBERT LOUIS STEVENSON

Requiem

Under the wide and starry sky,
Dig the grave and let me lie.
Glad did I live and gladly die,
   And I laid me down with a will.

This be the verse you grave for me:
Here he lies where he longed to be,
Home is the sailor, home from sea,
   And the hunter home from the hill.

When the Frost Is on the Punkin

When the frost is on the punkin and the fodder's in the
shock,
And you hear the kyouck and gobble of the struttin'
turkey-cock,
And the clackin' of the guineys, and the cluckin' of the
hens,
And the rooster's hallylooyer as he tiptoes on the fence;
Oh, it's then's the times a feller is a-feelin' at his best,
With the risin' sun to greet him from a night of peaceful
rest,
As he leaves the house, bareheaded, and goes out to feed
the stock,
When the frost is on the punkin and the fodder's in the
shock.

They's something kind o' harty-like about the atmusfere
When the heat of summer's over and the coolin' fall is
here.—
Of course we miss the flowers, and the blossoms on the
trees,
And the mumble of the hummin'-birds and buzzin' of the
bees;
But the air's so appetizin', and the landscape through the haze
Of a crisp and sunny morning of the airly autumn days
Is a pictur' that no painter has the colorin' to mock,—
When the frost is on the punkin and the fodder's in the
shock.

The husky, rusty russel of the tossels of the corn,
And the raspin' of the tangled leaves, as golden as the
morn;
The stubble in the furries—kind o' lonesome-like, but
still
A-preachin' sermuns to us of the barns they growed to fill;
The straw-stack in the medder, and the reaper in the shed;
The hosses in theyr stalls below, the clover overhead,—
Oh, it sets my hart a-clickin' like the tickin' of a clock,
When the frost is on the punkin and the fodder's in the
shock!

Then your apples all is gethered, and the ones a feller
keeps
Is poured around the celler-floor in red and yeller heaps;
And your cider-makin' 's over, and your wimmern-folks is
through
With their mince and apple butter, and theyr souse and
saussage, too! . . .
I don't know how to tell it—but ef sich a thing could be
As the Angels wantin' boardin', and they'd call around on
me—
I'd want to 'commodate 'em—all the whole-indurin'
flock—
When the frost is on the punkin and the fodder's in the
shock!

109 OSCAR WILDE

The Harlot's House

We caught the tread of dancing feet,
We loitered down the moonlit street,
And stopped beneath the harlot's house.

Inside, above the din and fray,
We heard the loud musicians play
The "Treues Liebes Herz" of Strauss.

Like strange mechanical grotesques,
Making fantastic arabesques,
The shadows raced across the blind.

We watched the ghostly dancers spin
To sound of horn and violin,
Like black leaves wheeling in the wind.

Like wire-pulled automatons,
Slim silhouetted skeletons
Went sidling through the slow quadrille.

They took each other by the hand,
And danced a stately saraband;
Their laughter echoed thin and shrill.

Sometimes a clockwork puppet pressed
A phantom lover to her breast,
Sometimes they seemed to try to sing.

Sometimes a horrible marionette
Came out, and smoked its cigarette
Upon the steps like a live thing.

Then, turning to my love, I said,
"The dead are dancing with the dead,
The dust is whirling with the dust."

But she—she heard the violin,
And left my side and entered in:
Love passed into the house of lust.

Then suddenly the tune went false,
The dancers wearied of the waltz,
The shadows ceased to wheel and whirl.

And down the long and silent street,
The dawn, with silver-sandaled feet,
Crept like a frightened girl.

A Runnable Stag

When the pods went pop on the broom, green broom,
And apples began to be golden-skinn'd,
We harbour'd a stag in the Priory coomb,
  And we feather'd his trail up-wind, up-wind,
  We feather'd his trail up-wind—
    A stag of warrant, a stag, a stag,
    A runnable stag, a kingly crop,
    Brow, bay and tray and three on top,
    A stag, a runnable stag.

Then the huntsman's horn rang yap, yap yap,
  And 'Forwards' we heard the harbourer shout;
But 'twas only a brocket that broke a gap
  In the beechen underwood, driven out,
  From the underwood antler'd out
    By warrant and might of the stag, the stag,
    The runnable stag, whose lordly mind
    Was bent on sleep, though beam'd and tined
    He stood, a runnable stag.

So we tufted the covert till afternoon
  With Tinkerman's Pup and Bell-of-the-North;
And hunters were sulky and hounds out of tune
  Before we tufted the right stag forth,
  Before we tufted him forth,
    The stag of warrant, the wily stag,
    The runnable stag with his kingly crop,

Brow, bay and tray and three on top,
The royal and runnable stag.

It was Bell-of-the-North and Tinkerman's Pup
That stuck to the scent till the copse was drawn.
'Tally ho! tally ho!' and the hunt was up,
The tufters whipp'd and the pack laid on,
The resolute pack laid on,
And the stag of warrant away at last,
The runnable stag, the same, the same,
His hoofs on fire, his horns like flame,
A stag, a runnable stag.

'Let your gelding be: if you check or chide
He stumbles at once and you're out of the hunt;
For three hundred gentlemen, able to ride,
On hunters accustom'd to bear the brunt,
Accustom'd to bear the brunt,
Are after the runnable stag, the stag,
The runnable stag with his kingly crop,
Brow, bay and tray and three on top,
The right, the runnable stag.'

By perilous paths in coomb and dell,
The heather, the rocks, and the river-bed,
The pace grew hot, for the scent lay well,
And a runnable stag goes right ahead,
The quarry went right ahead—
Ahead, ahead, and fast and far;
His antler'd crest, his cloven hoof,

Brow, bay and tray and three aloof,
The stag, the runnable stag.

For a matter of twenty miles and more,
By the densest hedge and the highest wall,
Through herds of bullocks he baffled the lore
Of harbourer, huntsman, hounds and all,
Of harbourer, hounds and all—
The stag of warrant, the wily stag,
For twenty miles, and five and five,
He ran, and he never was caught alive,
This stag, this runnable stag.

When he turn'd at bay in the leafy gloom,
In the emerald gloom where the brook ran deep
He heard in the distance the rollers boom,
And he saw in a vision of peaceful sleep
In a wonderful vision of sleep,
A stag of warrant, a stag, a stag,
A runnable stag in a jewell'd bed,
Under the sheltering ocean dead,
A stag, a runnable stag.

So a fateful hope lit up his eye,
And he open'd his nostrils wide again,
And he toss'd his branching antlers high
As he headed the hunt down the Charlock glen,
As he raced down the echoing glen—
For five miles more, the stag, the stag,
For twenty miles, and five and five,

Not to be caught now, dead or alive,
The stag, the runnable stag.

Three hundred gentlemen, able to ride,
Three hundred horses as gallant and free,
Beheld him escape on the evening tide,
Far out till he sank in the Severn Sea,
Till he sank in the depths of the sea—
The stag, the buoyant stag, the stag
That slept at last in a jewell'd bed
Under the sheltering ocean spread,
The stag, the runnable stag.

111 FRANCIS THOMPSON

The Hound of Heaven

I fled Him, down the nights and down the days:
  I fled Him, down the arches of the years:
I fled Him, down the labyrinthine ways
  Of my own mind; and in the mist of tears
I hid from Him, and under running laughter.
    Up vistaed hopes I sped;
    And shot, precipitated
Adown Titanic glooms of chasmed fears,
  From those strong Feet that followed, followed after.
    But with unhurrying chase,
    And unperturbèd pace,
  Deliberate speed, majestic instancy,
    They beat—and a Voice beat
    More instant than the Feet—
  "All things betray thee, who betrayest Me."

    I pleaded, outlaw-wise,
By many a hearted casement, curtained red,
  Trellised with intertwining charities;
(For, though I knew His Love Who followèd,
    Yet was I sore adread
Lest, having Him, I must have naught beside);
But, if one little casement parted wide,
  The gust of his approach would clash it to.
Fear wist not to evade, as Love wist to pursue.
Across the margent of the world I fled,
  And troubled the gold gateways of the stars,

Smiting for shelter on their clangèd bars;
Fretted to dulcet jars
And silver chatter the pale ports o' the moon.
I said to dawn, Be sudden; to eve, Be soon;
With thy young skiey blossoms heap me over
From this tremendous Lover!
Float thy vague veil about me, lest He see!
I tempted all his servitors, but to find
My own betrayal in their constancy,
In faith to Him their fickleness to me,
Their traitorous trueness, and their loyal deceit.
To all swift things for swiftness did I sue;
Clung to the whistling mane of every wind.
But whether they swept, smoothly fleet,
The long savannahs of the blue;
Or whether, Thunder-driven,
They clanged his chariot 'thwart a heaven
Plashy with flying lightnings round the spurn o'
their feet:—
Fear wist not to evade as Love wist to pursue.
Still with unhurrying chase,
And unperturbèd pace,
Deliberate speed, majestic instancy,
Came on the following Feet,
And a Voice above their beat—
"Naught shelters thee, who wilt not shelter Me."

I sought no more that after which I strayed
In face of man or maid;
But still within the little children's eyes
Seems something, something that replies;

They at least are for me, surely for me!
I turned me to them very wistfully;
But, just as their young eyes grew sudden fair
  With dawning answers there,
Their angel plucked them from me by the hair.
"Come then, ye other children, Nature's—share
With me" (said I) "your delicate fellowship;
  Let me greet you lip to lip,
  Let me twine with you caresses,
      Wantoning
    With our Lady-Mother's vagrant tresses,
      Banqueting
    With her in her wind-walled palace,
    Underneath her azured daïs,
    Quaffing, as your taintless way is,
      From a chalice
  Lucent-weeping out of the dayspring."
      So it was done:
  I in their delicate fellowship was one—
  Drew the bolt of Nature's secrecies.
  I knew all the swift importings
    On the wilful face of skies;
    I knew how the clouds arise
    Spumèd of the wild sea-snortings;
      All that's born or dies
    Rose and drooped with—made them shapers
  Of mine own moods, or wailful or divine—
    With them joyed and was bereaven.
    I was heavy with the even,
    When she lit her glimmering tapers
    Round the day's dead sanctities.

I laughed in the morning's eyes.
I triumphed and I saddened with all weather,
Heaven and I wept together,
And its sweet tears were salt with mortal mine;
Against the red throb of its sunset-heart
I laid my own to beat,
And share commingling heat;
But not by that, by that, was eased my human smart.
In vain my tears were wet on Heaven's grey cheek.
For ah! we know not what each other says,
These things and I; in sound *I* speak—
Their sound is but their stir, they speak by silences.
Nature, poor stepdame, cannot slake my drouth;
Let her, if she would owe me,
Drop yon blue bosom-veil of sky, and show me
The breasts o' her tenderness:
Never did any milk of hers once bless
My thirsting mouth.
Nigh and nigh draws the chase,
With unperturbèd pace,
Deliberate speed, majestic instancy;
And past those noisèd Feet
A voice comes yet more fleet—
"Lo! naught contents thee, who content'st not Me."

Naked I wait Thy love's uplifted stroke!
My harness piece by piece Thou hast hewn from me,
And smitten me to my knee;
I am defenceless utterly.
I slept, methinks, and woke,
And, slowly gazing, find me stripped in sleep.

In the rash lustihead of my young powers,
  I shook the pillaring hours
And pulled my life upon me; grimed with smears,
I stand amid the dust o' the mounded years—
My mangled youth lies dead beneath the heap.
My days have crackled and gone up in smoke,
Have puffed and burst as sun-starts on a stream.
  Yea, faileth now even dream
The dreamer, and the lute the lutanist;
Even the linked fantasies, in whose blossomy twist
I swung the earth a trinket at my wrist,
Are yielding; cores of all too weak account
For earth with heavy griefs so overplussed.
  Ah! is Thy love indeed
A weed, albeit an amaranthine weed,
Suffering no flowers except its own to mount?
  Ah! must—
  Designer infinite!—
Ah! must Thou char the wood ere Thou canst limn with it?
My freshness spent its wavering shower i' the dust;
And now my heart is as a broken fount,
Wherein tear-drippings stagnate, split down ever
  From the dank thoughts that shiver
Upon the sighful branches of my mind.
  Such is; what is to be?
The pulp so bitter, how shall taste the rind?
I dimly guess what Time in mists confounds;
Yet ever and anon a trumpet sounds
From the hid battlements of Eternity;
Those shaken mists a space unsettle, then
Round the half glimpsed turrets slowly wash again.

But not ere him who summoneth
I first have seen, enwound
With glooming robes purpureal, cypress-crowned;
His name I know, and what his trumpet saith.
Whether man's heart or life it be which yields
Thee harvest, must Thy harvest fields
Be dunged with rotten death?
Now of that long pursuit
Comes on at hand the bruit;
That Voice is round me like a bursting sea:
"And is thy earth so marred
Shattered in shard on shard?
Lo, all things fly thee, for thou fliest Me!
Strange, piteous, futile thing,
Wherefore should any set thee love apart?
Seeing none but I makes much of naught" (He said),
"And human love needs human meriting:
How hast thou merited—
Of all man's clotted clay the dingiest clot?
Alack, thou knowest not
How little worthy of any love thou art!
Whom wilt thou find to love ignoble thee
Save Me, save only Me?
All which I took from thee I did but take,
Not for thy harms,
But just that thou might'st seek it in My arms.
All which thy child's mistake
Fancies as lost, I have stored for thee at home:
Rise, clasp My hand, and come!"

Halts by me that footfall:

Is my gloom, after all,
Shade of His hand, outstretched caressingly?
"Ah, fondest, blindest, weakest,
I am He Whom thou seekest!
Thou dravest love from thee, who dravest Me."

112 ALFRED EDWARD HOUSMAN

'Is My Team Ploughing?'

'Is my team ploughing,
  That I was used to drive
And hear the harness jingle
  When I was man alive?'

Ay, the horses trample,
  The harness jingles now;
No change though you lie under
  The land you used to plough.

'Is football playing
  Along the river shore,
With lads to chase the leather,
  Now I stand up no more?'

Ay, the ball is flying,
  The lads play heart and soul,
The goal stands up, the keeper
  Stands up to keep the goal.

'Is my girl happy,
  That I thought hard to leave,
And has she tired of weeping
  As she lies down at eve?'

Ay, she lies down lightly,
  She lies not down to weep:

Your girl is well contented.
  Be still, my lad, and sleep.

'Is my friend hearty,
  Now I am thin and pine,
And has he found to sleep in
  A better bed than mine?'

Yes, lad, I lie easy,
  I lie as lads would choose;
I cheer a dead man's sweetheart,
  Never ask me whose.

113 BLISS CARMAN

The Joys of the Road

Now the joys of the road are chiefly these:
A crimson touch on the hard-wood trees;

A vagrant's morning wide and blue,
In early fall, when the wind walks, too;

A shadowy highway cool and brown
Alluring up and enticing down

From rippled water to dappled swamp,
From purple glory to scarlet pomp;

The outward eye, the quiet will,
And the striding heart from hill to hill;

The tempter apple over the fence;
The cobweb bloom on the yellow quince;

The palish asters along the wood,—
A lyric touch of the solitude;

An open hand, an easy shoe,
And a hope to make the day go through,—

Another to sleep with, and a third
To wake me up at the voice of a bird;

The resonant far-listening morn,
And the hoarse whisper of the corn;

The crickets mourning their comrades lost,
In the night's retreat from the gathering frost;

(Or is it their slogan, plaintive and shrill,
As they beat on their corselets, valiant still?)

A hunger fit for the kings of the sea,
And a loaf of bread for Dickon and me;

A thirst like that of the Thirsty Sword,
And a jug of cider on the board;

An idle noon, a bubbling spring,
The sea in the pine-tops murmuring;

A scrap of gossip at the ferry;
A comrade neither glum nor merry,

Asking nothing, revealing naught,
But minting his words from a fund of thought.

A keeper of silence eloquent,
Needy, yet royally well content,

Of the mettled breed, yet abhorring strife,
And full of the mellow juice of life,

A taster of wine, with an eye for a maid,
Never too bold, and never afraid,

Never heart-whole, never heart-sick,
(These are the things I worship in Dick)

No fidget and no reformer, just
A calm observer of ought and must,

A lover of books, but a reader of man,
No cynic and no charlatan,

Who never defers and never demands,
But, smiling, takes the world in his hands,—

Seeing it good as when God first saw
And gave it the weight of his will for law.

And O the joy that is never won,
But follows and follows the journeying sun,

By marsh and tide, by meadow and stream,
A will-o'-the-wind, a light-o'-dream,

Delusion afar, delight anear,
From morrow to morrow, from year to year,

A jack-o'-lantern, a fairy fire,
A dare, a bliss, and a desire!

The racy smell of the forest loam,
When the stealthy, sad-heart leaves go home;

(O leaves, O leaves, I am one with you,
Of the mould and the sun and the wind and the dew!)

The broad gold wake of the afternoon;
The silent fleck of the cold new moon;

The sound of the hollow sea's release
From stormy tumult to starry peace;

With only another league to wend;
And two brown arms at the journey's end!

These are the joys of the open road—
For him who travels without a load.

114 MARY ELIZABETH COLERIDGE

Unwelcome

We were young, we were merry, we were very very wise,
And the door stood open at our feast,
When there pass'd us a woman with the West in her eyes,
And a man with his back to the East.

O, still grew the hearts that were beating so fast,
The loudest voice was still.
The jest died away on our lips as they pass'd,
And the rays of July struck chill.

The cups of red wine turn'd pale on the board,
The white bread black as soot.
The hound forgot the hand of her lord,
She fell down at his foot.

Low let me lie, where the dead dog lies,
Ere I sit me down again at a feast,
When there passes a woman with the West in her eyes,
And a man with his back to the East.

115 RUDYARD KIPLING

Gunga Din

You may talk o' gin and beer
When you're quartered safe out 'ere,
An' you're sent to penny-fights an' Aldershot it;
But when it comes to slaughter
You will do your work on water,
An' you'll lick the bloomin' boots of 'im that's got it.
Now in Injia's sunny clime,
Where I used to spend my time
A-servin' of 'Er Majesty the Queen,
Of all them blackfaced crew
The finest man I knew
Was our regimental bhisti, Gunga Din.
He was "Din! Din! Din!
"You limpin' lump o' brick-dust, Gunga Din!
"Hi! Slippy *bitherao!*
"Water, get it! *Panee lao,*
"You squidgy-nosed old idol, Gunga Din."

The uniform 'e wore
Was nothin' much before,
An' rather less than 'arf o' that be'ind,
For a piece o' twisty rag
An' a goatskin water-bag
Was all the field-equipment 'e could find.
When the sweatin' troop-train lay
In a sidin' through the day,
Where the 'eat would make your bloomin' eyebrows crawl,

We shouted "Harry By!"
Till our throats were bricky-dry,
Then we wopped 'im 'cause 'e couldn't serve us all.
        It was "Din! Din! Din!
    "You 'eathen, where the mischief 'ave you been?
        "You put some *juidee* in it
        "Or I'll *marrow* you this minute
    "If you don't fill up my helmet, Gunga Din!"

'E would dot an' carry one
Till the longest day was done;
An' 'e didn't seem to know the use o' fear.
If we charged or broke or cut,
You could bet your bloomin' nut,
'E'd be waitin' fifty paces right flank rear.
With 'is mussick on 'is back,
'E would skip with our attack,
An' watch us till the bugles made "Retire,"
An' for all 'is dirty 'ide
'E was white, clear white, inside
When 'e went to tend the wounded under fire!
        It was "Din! Din! Din!"
    With the bullets kickin' dust-spots on the green,
        When the cartridges ran out,
        You could hear the front-ranks shout,
    "Hi! ammunition-mules an' Gunga Din!"

I shan't forgit the night
When I dropped be'ind the fight
With a bullet where my belt-plate should 'a' been.
I was chokin' mad with thirst,

An' the man that spied me first
Was our good old grinnin', gruntin' Gunga Din.
'E lifted up my 'ead,
An' he plugged me where I bled,
An' 'e guv me 'arf-a-pint o' water green.
It was crawlin' and it stunk,
But of all the drinks I've drunk,
I'm gratefullest to one from Gunga Din.
        It was "Din! Din! Din!
    " 'Ere's a beggar with a bullet through 'is spleen;
        " 'E's chawin' up the ground,
        "An' 'e's kickin' all around:
    "For Gawd's sake git the water, Gunga Din!"

'E carried me away
To where a dooli lay,
An' a bullet come an' drilled the beggar clean.
'E put me safe inside,
An' just before 'e died,
"I 'ope you liked your drink," sez Gunga Din.
So I'll meet 'im later on
At the place where 'e is gone—
Where it's always double drill and no canteen,
'E'll be squattin' on the coals
Givin' drink to poor damned souls,
An' I'll get a swig in hell from Gunga Din!
        Yes, Din! Din! Din!
    You Lazarushian-leather Gunga Din!
        Though I've belted you and flayed you,
        By the livin' Gawd that made you,
    You're a better man than I am, Gunga Din!

The Second Coming

Turning and turning in the widening gyre
The falcon cannot hear the falconer;
Things fall apart; the centre cannot hold;
Mere anarchy is loosed upon the world,
The blood-dimmed tide is loosed, and everywhere
The ceremony of innocence is drowned;
The best lack all conviction, while the worst
Are full of passionate intensity.

Surely some revelation is at hand;
Surely the Second Coming is at hand.
The Second Coming! Hardly are those words out
When a vast image out of *Spiritus Mundi*
Troubles my sight: somewhere in sands of the desert
A shape with lion body and the head of a man,
A gaze blank and pitiless as the sun,
Is moving its slow thighs, while all about it
Reel shadows of the indignant desert birds.
The darkness drops again; but now I know
That twenty centuries of stony sleep
Were vexed to nightmare by a rocking cradle,
And what rough beast, its hour come round at last,
Slouches towards Bethlehem to be born?

117 ERNEST DOWSON

Cynara

Last night, ah, yesternight, betwixt her lips and mine
There fell thy shadow, Cynara! thy breath was shed
Upon my soul between the kisses and the wine;
And I was desolate and sick of an old passion,
  Yea, I was desolate and bow'd my head:
I have been faithful to thee, Cynara! in my fashion.

All night upon mine heart I felt her warm heart beat,
Night-long within mine arms in love and sleep she lay;
Surely the kisses of her bought red mouth were sweet;
But I was desolate and sick of an old passion,
  When I awoke and found the dawn was gray:
I have been faithful to thee, Cynara! in my fashion.

I have forgot much, Cynara! gone with the wind,
Flung roses, roses, riotously with the throng,
Dancing, to put thy pale lost lilies out of mind;
But I was desolate and sick of an old passion,
  Yea, all the time, because the dance was long:
I have been faithful to thee, Cynara! in my fashion.

I cried for madder music and for stronger wine,
But when the feast is finish'd and the lamps expire,
Then falls thy shadow, Cynara! the night is thine;
And I am desolate and sick of an old passion,
  Yea, hungry for the lips of my desire:
I have been faithful to thee, Cynara! in my fashion.

118 EDWIN ARLINGTON ROBINSON

Mr. Flood's Party

Old Eben Flood, climbing alone one night
Over the hill between the town below
And the forsaken upland hermitage
That held as much as he should ever know
On earth again of home, paused warily.
The road was his with not a native near:
And Eben, having leisure, said aloud,
For no man else in Tilbury Town to hear:

"Well, Mr. Flood, we have the harvest moon
Again, and we may not have many more;
The bird is on the wing, the poet says,
And you and I have said it here before.
Drink to the bird." He raised up to the light
The jug that he had gone so far to fill,
And answered huskily: "Well, Mr. Flood,
Since you propose it, I believe I will."

Alone, as if enduring to the end
A valiant armor of scarred hopes outworn,
He stood there in the middle of the road
Like Roland's ghost winding a silent horn.
Below him, in the town among the trees,
Where friends of other days had honored him,
A phantom salutation of the dead
Rang thinly till old Eben's eyes were dim.

Then, as a mother lays her sleeping child
Down tenderly, fearing it may awake,
He set the jug down slowly at his feet
With trembling care, knowing that most things break;
And only when assured that on firm earth
It stood, as the uncertain lives of men
Assuredly did not, he paced away,
And with his hand extended paused again:

"Well, Mr. Flood, we have not met like this
In a long time; and many a change has come
To both of us, I fear, since last it was
We had a drop together. Welcome home!"
Convivially returning with himself,
Again he raised the jug up to the light;
And with an acquiescent quaver said:
"Well, Mr. Flood, if you insist, I might.

"Only a very little, Mr. Flood—
For auld lang syne. No more, sir; that will do."
So, for the time, apparently it did,
And Eben evidently thought so too;
For soon amid the silver loneliness
Of night he lifted up his voice and sang,
Secure, with only two moons listening,
Until the whole harmonious landscape rang—

"For auld lang syne." The weary throat gave out,
The last word wavered, and the song was done.
He raised again the jug regretfully
And shook his head, and was again alone.

There was not much that was ahead of him,
And there was nothing in the town below—
Where strangers would have shut the many doors
That many friends had opened long ago.

119 WILLIAM HENRY DAVIES

Leisure

What is this life if, full of care,
We have no time to stand and stare.

No time to stand beneath the boughs
And stare as long as sheep or cows.

No time to see, when woods we pass,
Where squirrels hide their nuts in grass.

No time to see, in broad daylight,
Streams full of stars, like skies at night.

No time to turn at Beauty's glance,
And watch her feet, how they can dance.

No time to wait till her mouth can
Enrich that smile her eyes began.

A poor life this if, full of care,
We have not time to stand and stare.

120 RALPH HODGSON

Eve

Eve, with her basket, was
Deep in the bells and grass,
Wading in bells and grass
Up to her knees,
Picking a dish of sweet
Berries and plums to eat,
Down in the bells and grass
Under the trees.

Mute as a mouse in a
Corner the cobra lay,
Curled round a bough of the
Cinnamon tall . . .
Now to get even and
Humble proud heaven and
Now was the moment or
Never at all.

"Eva!" Each syllable
Light as a flower fell,
"Eva!" he whispered the
Wondering maid,
Soft as a bubble sung
Out of a linnet's lung,
Soft and most silverly
"Eva!" he said.

Picture that orchard sprite,
Eve, with her body white,
Supple and smooth to her
Slim finger tips,
Wondering, listening,
Listening, wondering,
Eve with a berry
Half-way to her lips.

Oh had our simple Eve
Seen through the make-believe!
Had she but known the
Pretender he was!
Out of the boughs he came,
Whispering still her name,
Tumbling in twenty rings
Into the grass.

Here was the strangest pair
In the world anywhere,
Eve in the bells and grass
Kneeling, and he
Telling his story low . . .
Singing birds saw them go
Down the dark path to
The Blasphemous Tree.

Oh what a clatter when
Titmouse and Jenny Wren
Saw him successful and
Taking his leave!

How the birds rated him,
How they all hated him!
How they all pitied
Poor motherless Eve!

Picture her crying
Outside in the lane,
Eve, with no dish of sweet
Berries and plums to eat,
Haunting the gate of the
Orchard in vain . . .
Picture the lewd delight
Under the hill to-night—
"Eva!" the toast goes round,
"Eva!" again.

121 WALTER DE LA MARE

The Listeners

"Is there anybody there?" said the Traveller,
  Knocking on the moonlit door;
And his horse in the silence champed the grasses
  Of the forest's ferny floor:
And a bird flew up out of the turret,
  Above the Traveller's head:
And he smote upon the door again a second time;
  "Is there anybody there?" he said.
But no one descended to the Traveller;
  No head from the leaf-fringed sill
Leaned over and looked into his grey eyes,
  Where he stood perplexed and still.
But only a host of phantom listeners
  That dwelt in the lone house then
Stood listening in the quiet of the moonlight
  To that voice from the world of men:
Stood thronging the faint moon beams on the dark stair,
  That goes down to the empty hall,
Hearkening in an air stirred and shaken
  By the lonely traveller's call.
And he felt in his heart their strangeness,
  Their stillness answering his cry,
While his horse moved, cropping the dark turf,
  'Neath the starred and leafy sky;
For he suddenly smote on the door, even
  Louder, and lifted his head:—
"Tell them I came, and no one answered,

That I kept my word," he said.
Never the least stir made the listeners,
Though every word he spake
Fell echoing through the shadowiness of the still house
From the one man left awake:
Ay, they heard his foot upon the stirrup,
And the sound of iron on stone
And how the silence surged softly backward
When the plunging hoofs were gone.

122 ROBERT FROST

Stopping by Woods on a Snowy Evening

Whose woods these are I think I know.
His house is in the village though;
He will not see me stopping here
To watch his woods fill up with snow.

My little horse must think it queer
To stop without a farmhouse near
Between the woods and frozen lake
The darkest evening of the year.

He gives his harness bells a shake
To ask if there is some mistake.
The only other sound's the sweep
Of easy wind and downy flake.

The woods are lovely, dark and deep.
But I have promises to keep,
And miles to go before I sleep,
And miles to go before I sleep.

123 JOHN MASEFIELD

Cargoes

Quinquireme of Nineveh from distant Ophir
Rowing home to haven in sunny Palestine,
With a cargo of ivory,
And apes and peacocks,
Sandalwood, cedarwood, and sweet white wine.

Stately Spanish galleon coming from the Isthmus,
Dipping through the Tropics by the palm-green shores,
With a cargo of diamonds,
Emeralds, amethysts,
Topazes, and cinnamon, and gold moidores.

Dirty British coaster with a salt-caked smoke stack
Butting through the Channel in the mad March days,
With a cargo of Tyne coal,
Road-rail, pig-lead,
Firewood, iron-ware, and cheap tin trays.

124 EDWARD THOMAS

Adlestrop

Yes. I remember Adlestrop—
The name, because one afternoon
Of heat the express-train drew up there
Unwontedly. It was late June.

The steam hiss'd. Some one clear'd his throat.
No one left and no one came
On the bare platform. What I saw
Was Adlestrop—only the name

And willows, willow-herb, and grass,
And meadowsweet, and haycocks dry,
No whit less still and lonely fair
Than the high cloudlets in the sky.

And for that minute a blackbird sang
Close by, and round him, mistier,
Farther and farther, all the birds
Of Oxfordshire and Gloucestershire.

125 SIEGFRIED SASSOON

Everyone Sang

Everyone suddenly burst out singing;
And I was fill'd with such delight
As prison'd birds must find in freedom
Winging wildly across the white
Orchards and dark-green fields; on; on; and out of
sight.

Everyone's voice was suddenly lifted,
And beauty came like the setting sun.
My heart was shaken with tears; and horror
Drifted away . . . O but every one
Was a bird; and the song was wordless; the
singing will never be done.

The Horses

Barely a twelvemonth after
The seven days war that put the world to sleep.
Late in the evening the strange horses came.
By then we had made our covenant with silence,
But in the first few days it was so still
We listened to our breathing and were afraid.
On the second day
The radios failed: we turned the knobs; no answer.
On the third day a warship passed us, heading north,
Dead bodies piled on the deck. On the sixth day
A plane plunged over us into the sea. Thereafter
Nothing. The radios dumb;
And still they stand in corners of our kitchens,
And stand, perhaps, turned on, in a million rooms
All over the world. But now if they should speak,
If on a sudden they should speak again,
If on the stroke of noon a voice should speak,
We would not listen, we would not let it bring
That old bad world that swallowed its children quick
At one great gulp. We would not have it again.
Sometimes we think of the nations lying asleep,
Curled blindly in impenetrable sorrow,
And then the thought confounds us with its strangeness.
The tractors lie about our fields; at evening
They look like dank sea-monsters couched and waiting.
We leave them where they are and let them rust:
"They'll molder away and be like other loam."

We make our oxen drag our rusty plows,
Long laid aside. We have gone back
Far past our fathers' land.

And then, that evening
Late in the summer the strange horses came.
We heard a distant tapping on the road,
A deepening drumming: it stopped, went on again
And at the corner changed to hollow thunder.
We saw the heads
Like a wild wave charging and were afraid.
We had sold our horses in our fathers' time
To buy new tractors. Now they were strange to us
As fabulous steeds set on an ancient shield
Or illustrations in a book of knights.
We did not dare go near them. Yet they waited,
Stubborn and shy, as if they had been sent
By an old command to find our whereabouts
And that long-lost archaic companionship.
In the first moment we had never a thought
That they were creatures to be owned and used.
Among them were some half a dozen colts
Dropped in some wilderness of the broken world,
Yet new as if they had come from their own Eden.
Since then they have pulled our plows and borne our loads.
But that free servitude still can pierce our hearts.
Our life is changed: their coming our beginning.

127 ROBINSON JEFFERS

The Eye

The Atlantic is a stormy moat; and the Mediterranean
The blue pool in the old garden,
More than five thousand years has drunk sacrifice
Of ships and blood, and shines in the sun; but here the
Pacific—
Our ships, planes, wars are perfectly irrelevant.
Neither our present blood-feud with the brave dwarfs
Nor any future world-quarrel of westering
And eastering man, the bloody migrations, greed of
power, clash of faiths—
Is a speck of dust on the great scale-pan.
Here from this mountain shore, headland beyond stormy
headland
plunging like dolphins through the blue sea-smoke
Into pale sea—look west at the hill of water: it is half the
planet: this dome, this half-globe, this bulging
Eyeball of water, arched over to Asia,
Australia and white Antarctica: those are the eyelids that
never close; this is the staring unsleeping
Eye of the earth; and what it watches is not our wars.

Strange Meeting

It seemed that out of battle I escaped
Down some profound dull tunnel, long since scooped
Through granites which titanic wars had groined.
Yet also there encumbered sleepers groaned,
Too fast in thought or death to be bestirred.
Then, as I probed them, one sprang up, and stared
With piteous recognition in fixed eyes,
Lifting distressful hands as if to bless.
And by his smile, I knew that sullen hall;
By his dead smile I knew we stood in Hell.
With a thousand pains that vision's face was grained;
Yet no blood reached there from the upper ground,
And no guns thumped, or down the flues made moan.
"Strange friend," I said, "here is no cause to mourn."
"None," said the other, "save the undone years,
The hopelessness. Whatever hope is yours,
Was my life also; I went hunting wild
After the wildest beauty in the world,
Which lies not calm in eyes, or braided hair,
But mocks the steady running of the hour,
And if it grieves, grieves richlier than here.
For by my glee might many men have laughed,
And of my weeping something had been left,
Which must die now. I mean the truth untold,
The pity of war, the pity war distilled.
Now men will go content with what we spoiled,
Or, discontent, boil bloody, and be spilled.

They will be swift with swiftness of the tigress,
None will break ranks, though nations trek from progress.
Courage was mine, and I had mystery,
Wisdom was mine, and I had mastery;
To miss the march of this retreating world
Into vain citadels that are not walled.
Then when much blood had clogged their chariot wheels
I would go up and wash them from sweet wells,
Even with truths that lie too deep for taint.
I would have poured my spirit without stint
But not through wounds; not on the cess of war.
Foreheads of men have bled where no wounds were.
I am the enemy you killed, my friend.
I knew you in this dark; for so you frowned
Yesterday through me as you jabbed and killed.
I parried; but my hands were loath and cold.
Let us sleep now . . . ."

129 HART CRANE

Voyages. II

And yet this great wink of eternity,
Of runless floods, unfettered leewardings,
Samite sheeted and processioned where
Her undinal vast belly moonward bends,
Laughing the wrapped inflections of our love;

Take this Sea, whose diapason knells
On scrolls of silver snowy sentences,
The sceptred terror of whose sessions rends
As her demeanors motion well or ill,
All but the pieties of lovers' hands.

And onward, as bells off San Salvador
Salute the crocus lustres of the stars,
In these poinsettia meadows of her tides,—
Adagios of islands, O my Prodigal,
Complete the dark confessions her veins spell.

Mark how her turning shoulders wind the hours,
And hasten while her penniless rich palms
Pass superscription of bent foam and wave,—
Hasten, while they are true,—sleep, death, desire,
Close round one instant in one floating flower.

Bind us in time, O Seasons clear, and awe.
O minstrel galleons of Carib fire,
Bequeath us to no earthly shore until
Is answered in the vortex of our grave
The seal's wide spindrift gaze toward paradise.

130 DYLAN THOMAS

Do Not Go Gentle into That Good Night

Do not go gentle into that good night,
Old age should burn and rave at close of day;
Rage, rage against the dying of the light.

Though wise men at their end know dark is right,
Because their words had forked no lightning they
Do not go gentle into that good night.

Good men, the last wave by, crying how bright
Their frail deeds might have danced in a green bay,
Rage, rage against the dying of the light.

Wild men who caught and sang the sun in flight,
And learn, too late, they grieved it on its way,
Do not go gentle into that good night.

Grave men, near death, who see with blinding sight
Blind eyes could blaze like meteors and be gay,
Rage, rage against the dying of the light.

And you, my father, there on the sad height,
Curse, bless, me now with your fierce tears, I pray.
Do not go gentle into that good night.
Rage, rage against the dying of the light.

PUBLISHER'S AFTERWORD

Make the ordinary extraordinary.

These four words express the purpose and value of poetry better, perhaps, than any others. They have been repeated over the years by Lucien Stryk for the thousands of individuals to whom he has introduced the wonder of great poetry.

That these poems have endured and have continued to make the ordinary extraordinary gives them timelessness. That these poems have become a part of our lives gives them great value in the way family heirlooms are cherished by many generations. These are the treasured poems, the poetry of common people, the great works that give us brief, extraordinary moments in an otherwise ordinary passage.

The selection of Lucien Stryk to collect and introduce the poetry for this book recognizes one of the world's most extraordinary poets and teachers. Few who travel this way are fortunate enough to encounter one extraordinary individual who possesses the wisdom and understanding to change—for all time—our lives. Lucien Stryk is one of those true masters. Through his poetry and his life, he has made ordinary people extraordinary and he has created rare essences of better worlds.

As a poet, Lucien Stryk has become like the poems collected in this volume: timeless, treasured, vital and clear, formed pure in wisdom and understanding. Like the poems collected, he has attained the rarest of all states of existence: he has entered the world memory.

The collection of poetry you hold is a gift. It is a gift of the poets, and it is a gift of the thousands who return often to these poems and pass them to succeeding generations. It is a lasting gift of extraordinary value and importance in our complex, unsettled world. Above all, it is a gift of the simple joy and pleasure that great, familiar poetry brings to our lives, a gift made possible by the generous support of Eugene J. Metzger and his belief that a book of great poems by great poets will always have a place in a great America.

Index of First Lines

Grateful acknowledgement is made to the following for permission to reprint previously published material:

Crane, Hart; *Voyages. II*: From THE COMPLETE POEMS AND SELECTED LETTERS AND PROSE OF HART CRANE, Edited by Brom Weber. Copyright 1933, 1958, 1966 by Liveright Publishing Corporation. Reprinted with the permission of Liveright Publishing Corporation.

de la Mare, Walter, *The Listeners*: From COLLECTED POEMS by Walter de la Mare. Copyright 1941 by Walter de la Mare. Reprinted by permission of Henry Holt and Company, Inc.; The Literary Trustees of Walter de la Mare; and The Society of Authors as their representative.

Frost, Robert; *Stopping by Woods on a Snowy Evening:* From THE POETRY OF ROBERT FROST edited by Edward Connery Lathem. Copyright 1923, © 1969 by Holt, Rinehart and Winston. Copyright 1951 by Robert Frost. Reprinted by permission of Henry Holt and Company, Inc.

Hardy, Thomas; *The Darkling Thrush*: From THE COMPLETE POEMS OF THOMAS HARDY edited by James Gibson. Copyright 1978 by Macmillin Publishing Company. Reprinted with permission of Macmillan Publishing Company.

Housman, Alfred Edward; *'Is My Team Ploughing'*: From COLLECTED POEMS OF A. E. HOUSMAN by A. E. Housman. Copyright 1939, 1940, © 1965 by Holt, Rinehart and Winston. Copyright © 1967, 1968 by Robert E. Symons. Reprinted by permission of Henry Holt and Company, Inc.

Jeffers, Robinson; *The Eye*: From THE SELECTED POETRY OF ROBINSON JEFFERS by Robinson Jeffers. Copyright 1941, 1944, and renewed 1969, 1972 by Donnan Jeffers and Garth Jeffers. Reprinted by permission of Random House, Inc.

Masefield, John; *Cargoes*: From THE COLLECTED POEMS OF JOHN MASEFIELD by John Masefield. Reprinted by permission of The Society of Authors as the literary representative of the Estate of John Masefield.

Muir, Edwin; *The Horses*: From COLLECTED POEMS by Edwin Muir. Reprinted by permission of Faber and Faber, Ltd. and Oxford University Press.

Owen, Wilfred: *Strange Meeting*: From POEMS, by Wilfred Owen. Reprinted with the permission of New Directions Publishing Company.

Robinson, Edwin Arlington; *Mr. Flood's Party*: From COLLECTED POEMS OF EDWARD ARLINGTON ROBINSON. Copyright 1921 by Edwin Arlington Robinson, renewed 1949 by Ruth Nivison. Reprinted with permission of Macmillan Publishing Company.

Sassoon, Siegfried; *Everyone Sang*: From COLLECTED POEMS by Siegfried Sassoon. Copyright 1918, 1920 by E. P. Dutton, copyright 1936, 1946, 1947, 1948 by Siegfried Sassoon. Reprinted by permission of Viking Penguin, A Division of Viking Books USA Inc.

Thomas, Dylan; *Do Not Go Gentle Into that Good Night*: From COLLECTED POEMS OF DYLAN THOMAS. Reprinted with the permission of New Directions Publishing Company and David Higham, Limited.

Yeats, William Butler; *The Second Coming*: From THE POEMS OF W. B. YEATS: A NEW EDITION edited by Richard J. Finneran. Copyright 1924 by Macmillan Publishing Company, renewed 1952 by Bertha Georgie Yeats.

THE GIFT OF GREAT POETRY

Designed by Christine Swirnoff

Composed by Pagesetters Inc., Brattleboro, Vermont

Set in Caslon 540

Printed and Bound by

R. R. Donnelley & Sons, Crawfordsville, Indiana